Leading with Technologies

Leading with Technologies

Improving Performance for Educators

Edited by
Gary Ivory and Dana Christman

ROWMAN & LITTLEFIELD
Lanham • Boulder • New York • London

Published by Rowman & Littlefield
An imprint of The Rowman & Littlefield Publishing Group, Inc.
4501 Forbes Boulevard, Suite 200, Lanham, Maryland 20706
www.rowman.com

6 Tinworth Street, London SE11 5AL, United Kingdom

Copyright © 2019 by Gary Ivory and Dana Christman

All rights reserved. No part of this book may be reproduced in any form or by any electronic or mechanical means, including information storage and retrieval systems, without written permission from the publisher, except by a reviewer who may quote passages in a review.

British Library Cataloguing in Publication Information Available

Library of Congress Cataloging-in-Publication Data Available

ISBN: 978-1-4758-1117-9 (cloth : alk. paper)
ISBN: 978-1-4758-1118-6 (pbk. : alk. paper)
ISBN: 978-1-4758-1119-3 (electronic)

∞™ The paper used in this publication meets the minimum requirements of American National Standard for Information Sciences—Permanence of Paper for Printed Library Materials, ANSI/NISO Z39.48-1992.

Contents

Foreword *John B. Nash*	ix
Preface *Gary Ivory & Dana Christman*	xiii
Question 1: What Do We Want From Education?	xiii
Question 2: Why Do We Believe Education Leadership Is Key to Getting What We Want?	xiv
Question 3: What Kinds of Leaders Do We Need for Education?	xv
Question 4: How Might We Think About the Place of Technology in Education?	xvi
Overview of the Book	xviii
References	xix
Acknowledgments	xxi

1 The Right Information When You Need It: The iPad and iBooks   1
   Kevin Badgett

Key Points in This Chapter	1
Technology and School Leadership: Efficiency Tools	1
Overcoming Our Resistance to Technology	1
Research and Tools: iBooks	2
Decisions Informed by Regulations	4
Cautions	6

	Conclusion	6
	References	7
2	**The Qualitative Side of Data-Driven Leadership: Using Computer-Assisted Qualitative Data Analysis Software to Inform and Guide Leadership Practice** *Chad R. Lochmiller & Jessica N. Lester*	9
	Key Points in This Chapter	9
	Understanding the Qualitative Side of Data-Driven Leadership	10
	Qualitative Data Sources and the Qualitative Data Analysis Process	12
	Analyzing Qualitative Data	13
	Computer-Assisted Qualitative-Data-Analysis Software (CAQDAS)	13
	ATLAS.ti for the iPad: A Supportive Technology Tool for Educational Leaders	14
	Examples From Practice	18
	Analyzing Student Work at Stoneybrook Elementary	18
	Observing Classroom Instruction and Student Engagement at Westminster High School	20
	Improving Principal Support in the District Office at Hillsdale School District	21
	Conclusions	23
	Note	23
	References	23
3	***Classwalk*: A Tool to Enhance Instructional Leadership** *Sharon Wilbur, Sharon Dean, Leslie Williams, Linda Atkinson, & Jean Cate*	25
	Key Points in This Chapter	25
	A Case for Walkthroughs	25
	Classwalk	27
	Four Functions of *Classwalk*	27
	Function 1: Teachers (Figure 3.2)	28
	Function 2: Templates (Figure 3.3)	29
	Function 3: Walkthrough	32
	Function 4: Analysis (Figures 3.8 and 3.9)	33
	Using Walkthrough Data	35
	Worth the Time	35
	Causal Data Versus Symptoms Data	36
	Conclusion	37
	References	37

4 Technology to Enhance Comprehensive Communication   39
Jon Tienhaara, David Wicks, & Thomas Alsbury

Key Points in This Chapter	39
ISTE Standards for Education Leaders	40
ISTE Standard 3: Empowering Learning	40
ISTE Standard 2: Visionary Planner	40
Data Collection	41
Case Scenario 1: Preparing for the New School Year	41
Application of Technology to Case Scenario 1	43
Practical Application of Web Forms for the School Administrator	45
Collaborative Writing	46
Case Scenario 2: Teacher Collaboration	47
Application of Technology to Case Scenario 2	47
Practical Application of Cloud Documents for the School Administrator	49
Communication	50
Case Scenario 3: Improved Communication	50
Application of Technology to Case Scenario 3	50
Practical Application of Internet Communication for the School Administrator	52
Matters of Privacy	53
Conclusion	53
References	54

5 Searching, Curating, and Networking: Set Up the Tools and Develop the Skills to Make the Modern Web Work for You   55
Julia L. Parra

Key Points in This Chapter	55
Part 1: Set Up Your Toolkit	56
Get Started with Google/Google Search	57
Get Started with Twitter	58
Get Started with Facebook	60
Get Started with Pinterest	61
Part 2: Develop Three Key Skills—Searching, Curating, and Networking	62
Skill 1: Searching for Information and Resources	62
Administrative Scenario: Searching for Resources for Your Upcoming Professional Development Meeting	63
Google It	63

Twitter Search	64
Facebook Search	65
Skill 2: Curating the Great Resources You Are Finding	66
Administrative Scenario: Curating the Resources for Your Upcoming PD Meeting	66
Curate with Pinterest	66
Skill 3: Networking for Professional Growth	68
Administrative Scenario: Networking for Professional Growth	72
Conclusion	73
References	74

6 Legal Issues for Educators in Using Technology and Social Media   77
Robert F. Hachiya

Key Points in This Chapter	77
Social Media and the Speech Rights of Educators	78
Political or Policy Commentary on Social Media	78
Suggested Policy and Practice Related to Educators and Social Media	81
Advice Regarding Professional and Personal Social Media	81
Conclusion	82
References	82
Glossary	85
Index	89
About the Contributors	95
About the Reviewers	97

Foreword
John B. Nash

Perhaps you will indulge me as I tell a story. The story is about technology, but not of the computing kind (at least not initially). While contemplating how to write this, my mind turned to the bicycle. In the spring of 1973, S. S. Wilson published an article in *Scientific American* titled "Bicycle Technology." In this piece, Wilson chronicled in fascinating historical detail the mechanical iterations that have led to what we conceive of as the modern bike. Two aspects of Wilson's article struck me in particular.

One is that like the computer, the bicycle is a relatively recent invention. As Wilson notes, "[When] one considers how long the wheel has served in transportation (more than 5,000 years), it seems odd that the first really effective self-propelled wheeled vehicle was developed only about 100 years ago" (Wilson, 1973, p. 82).

The second thing that struck me is a bicycle's properties in terms of how it allows humans to move about in a way that "quite outdoes human evolution" (Wilson, 1973, p. 82). You see, it is possible to calculate the energy consumed in moving across any distance as a function of weight, whether we're talking about an animal or a machine. For humans, an unaided person is in the quadrant that performs fairly well (jets, horses, and salmon fare better; mice, fruit flies, and lemmings are among the most inefficient).

However, when a human is on a bike, things change dramatically. In essence, if you place a human on a bicycle, the human's overall weight only goes up a little but the cost of moving, as measured by calories per gram per kilometer, drops dramatically. In fact, the cyclist is number one in efficiency "among moving creatures and machines" (Wilson, 1973, p. 82). That is an impressive statistic. It's this second bit, how bicycle technology allows humans to move about in ways that outdo human evolution, that had me thinking about computer technology. Enter Steve Jobs into the story.

In the spring of 1981, Apple Computer cofounder and CEO, Steve Jobs, then 26, appeared on the ABC News program *Nightline* for one of his first nationally broadcast news interviews. Jobs and a writer named David Burnham debated the seriousness of privacy concerns raised by the increasing pervasiveness of computers in society. Recall that in 1981, the personal computing revolution was just getting underway. At one point in the interview the anchor, Ted Koppel, asked Jobs why he considered the computer to be the "bicycle of the 21st century." Here is what Jobs said:

> Well actually I read a survey in *Scientific American* in the early 70s and what this survey had done was it measured the efficiency of locomotion for various species of things on the planet—birds, fish, dogs—and it ranked them and it turned out that the condor won. The condor took the least amount of energy to get from point A to point B, and man sort of came in with a rather unimpressive showing about a third of the way down the list.
>
> But someone at that magazine had the insight to test the efficiency of man riding a bicycle. And man riding a bicycle is twice as good as the condor—all the way off the end of the list. And it really illustrated man's ability as a tool maker to fashion a tool to amplify an inherent ability that he has. And that's really exactly what we feel we're doing. We're really sort of blazing the trails for the 21st century bicycle, but to amplify a slightly different inherent ability that man has, the ability of a certain part of intelligence.
>
> Right now, we're at the mechanical part of intelligence where one of these devices can free a person from many of the drudgery of life and allow really humans to do what they do best which is to work on the conceptual level; to work on the creative level. (Newcomb, 2016)

It's hard not to believe Jobs was referring to Wilson's 1973 article, although having read it myself, I'm not exactly sure where he got the idea about the condor—which did not appear among the animals and machines noted by Wilson. But I can't help appreciating the analogy to the bicycle.

Consider the topics addressed by the authors of this book: information finding, data analysis, leading people, communication, cultivating expertise. All represent abilities inherent within humans and exhibited for millennia among complex civilizations. But this book considers these topics in the presence of computer technology. Thus the question may be, how are these abilities amplified by this tool? What value is accrued? Or, perhaps framed in terms of the bicycle, what might occur faster with less energy? There are several candidate answers, I'm sure, and I land on *insight*.

What is insight? It is the act of grasping the inner essence of things. It is the ability to see into a situation. Insight is a powerful state of knowing. And given that computing technology is so ubiquitous today, we may take for granted the amplification computers afford us in situations we may consider to be commonplace.

Take a common practice carried out by principals: the walkthrough. Principals could conduct walkthroughs on their own and record their observations through long-form notes that they later use for planning, improvement, or coaching. They might gain personal insight from that experience, but it would be on their shoulders to share that insight. They could ask others to join them on the walkthroughs and later discuss what each in the group saw and what each learned from it.

From this, the group might accrue insight, which might inform their work. The principals could invite others on the walkthroughs, and everyone in the group could record their observations by making marks with a pen on an agreed-upon observation form, which provides a platform for discussing the observations in a standard way. Insight could be gleaned from reviewing the forms over time.

Let's say, however, the principal invites others on the walkthrough, asks everyone to enter their observations into a tablet computer, and after a month's time the aggregate, anonymous data are displayed on a screen during a grade-level or faculty meeting where the professional learning staff are invited to be a part of interpreting the findings. They are asked questions such as "What do you notice?" and "Why do you think the data appear as they do?" Hypotheses are formed. Potential strategies are offered. A collective insight begins to be reached. And a human ability is amplified.

So, as you embark on the journey these authors have laid out for you, consider not only the features offered by the technologies. Consider how they extend that which makes you human. Think of them collectively as your bicycle outstripping the condor.

John B. Nash
Director of the University of Kentucky's Laboratory
on Design Thinking in Education
Associate Professor and Department Chair of Educational
Leadership Studies at the University of Kentucky
Lexington
April 2018

REFERENCES

Newcomb, Alyssa. (2016, April 1). Apple at 40: What Steve Jobs said about computers in 1981. Available from https://abcnews.go.com/Technology/apple-40-steve-jobs-computers-1981/story?id=38064087

Wilson, S. S. (1973, March). Bicycle technology. *Scientific American, 228,* 81–91. doi:10.1038/scientificamerican0373-81

Preface
Gary Ivory & Dana Christman

Over 20 years ago, a colleague of ours gave a presentation entitled, "If technology is the answer, what is the question?" What a great topic! Anyone who dares to produce a book called *Leading with Technologies* certainly ought to ponder it. We find that the question posed more than two decades ago remains relevant to us today.

We want, however, to make it plural, "If technology is the answer, what *are* the question*s*?" We offer four questions here:

1. What do we want from education?
2. Why do we believe education leadership is key to getting what we want?
3. What kinds of leaders do we need for education?
4. How might we think about the place of technology in education?

QUESTION 1: WHAT DO WE WANT FROM EDUCATION?

We preface our answer by stating that the two of us believe passionately in the value of learning. Learning, in one form or another, is simply one of the most positive enterprises to which humans can aspire. Learning enables us almost always to become better than we are.

In 2017, deans of colleges of education and the National Education Policy Center formulated a statement of principles about the condition of education in the United States. We cite it here to give our answer to the question, "What do we want from education?" This document emphasized the value of "a school system that serves all children and youth, providing them with richly engaging, challenging, and supported opportunities to learn" (Education Deans for Justice and Equity & National Education Policy Center, 2017, p. 2).

Their reference to "opportunities to learn" is similar to a purpose of schooling from Skrla, McKenzie, and Scheurich (2009): "Every learner—in whatever learning environment that learner is found—has the greatest opportunity to learn enhanced by the supports necessary to achieve competence, excellence, independence, responsibility, and self-sufficiency for school and for life" (p. 14). We adhere to the beliefs expressed in both documents.

QUESTION 2: WHY DO WE BELIEVE EDUCATION LEADERSHIP IS KEY TO GETTING WHAT WE WANT?

We have known teachers personally who did not believe leadership is key. They went into their classrooms, taught at high levels, developed good relationships with their students, fostered learning, and did this consistently year after year. They saw no reason to think the work of the principal or other leaders was relevant to their vitally important work of classroom instruction. Their implicit question was, "If the most important work of education goes on between me and my students, why should I need anyone to lead me?"

The two of us, however, as scholars of leadership, see organization as key to education. But why? Why should it be necessary for education to be organized? Answering this question throws us into the topic of the democratic society. If each of us is to live in freedom, if each of us is to participate in self-government, then each of us must have some competence to govern ourselves and some understanding of how to participate in self-government. A democratic society needs citizens who can govern themselves and who can participate wisely.

So society needs to develop those kinds of citizens. That is why society needs to educate. We believe organized efforts to educate are likely to produce results more consistently than random efforts. That is why we need organization and that is why we need leaders. We presented the aspirations of the Education Deans for Justice and Equity (2017) and those of Skrla et al. (2009) because they are also our aspirations for education, and we maintain that the ideal cannot be reached consistently merely by each individual teacher going into the classroom and teaching at a high level (though that is certainly an essential component in pursuit of the ideal).

Furthermore, the quotations from the education deans and from Skrla and her colleagues allude to systems and support, which makes us think of organizations. Pursuing the ideal for "every learner—in whatever environment" depends on an organization that will bring educators to work together for the ideal. And a well-run organization depends on good leaders.

Good leaders support efforts to establish a mission for the organization so that people and their efforts will tend to be focused on a small number of important goals. Leaders secure resources and put them where they are most needed. They inspire people to work together at a high level and hold accountable those who do not.

They monitor successes and setbacks to help organization members learn from them. Leaders keep their eyes out for problems that are hindering effectiveness and minimize the effects of the problems. They marshal support from their constituencies and from power holders who can affect the success of the organization for good or ill. We see these tasks of the leader as essential to providing opportunities to all learners.

In fact, a six-year study conducted with more than 1,000 educators (Seashore Louis, Leithwood, Wahlstrom, & Anderson, 2010) found, "Among all the parents, teachers, and policy makers who work hard to improve education, educators in leadership positions are uniquely well positioned to ensure the necessary synergy" (p. 9) in helping to improve educational practice and student learning. In all the data collected in this study, the research team did not find "a single case of a school improving its student achievement record in the absence of talented leadership" (p. 9).

QUESTION 3: WHAT KINDS OF LEADERS DO WE NEED FOR EDUCATION?

We believe education needs leaders who aspire to expertise. "Expertise" can be a daunting word. It can suggest the intense concentration of the world-class chess master, the flawless execution of an Olympic gymnast, or the inspiring performances of the highest-level artists. School leaders immersed in (even weary from) their hectic daily struggles may consider the call to expertise a hollow one.

You, as an education leader, may aspire to expertise in providing students "with richly engaging, challenging, and supported opportunities to learn" as the education deans said in the quote above. But at the same time, you may feel distracted by responsibilities to an assortment of people: students, teachers, parents, community members, other administrators and school district personnel, higher education institutions, and the public.

In particular, you must respond to pressures from a number of federal, state, regional, and local agencies outside of your schools and districts. Thus, while aspiring to the highest ideals, you may feel incredible pressure, like a juggler, to keep all the balls in the air (different-sized balls, of different weights, moving at different speeds).

Your performance, because it is so diffused and difficult to nail down, may never seem quite as impressive or awe-inspiring as that of the gymnast performing her one-minute floor exercise. The question of expertise may seem irrelevant to your life and work. Nevertheless we offer here a nontraditional definition of expertise, one that we believe is relevant to the work of the school leader, or in fact any leader. We present Bereiter and Scardamalia's (1993) definition of *expertise as a career*. In their definition, they contrast the career of the expert with that of the nonexpert:

> *The career of the expert is one of progressively advancing on the problems constituting a field of work, whereas the career of the nonexpert is one of gradually constricting the field of work so that it more closely conforms to the routines the nonexpert is prepared to execute.* (p. 11, emphasis in the original)

This view of expertise seems to us to throw a new light on the school leader. The point of expertise in this definition is not to win a medal, perform to cheering throngs, or get on the cover of *Time Magazine* (or even of the local paper). That is what experts earn in the traditional view.

Bereiter and Scardamalia's (1993) definition of expertise is useful in that (a) it allows for expertise in the real world, the world of the education leader, which is rarely about precision or flawless execution; (b) it provides a view of expertise that is relevant to your day-to-day life as a leader where there is rarely a specific performance that counts—rather, all of your words and actions can make a difference; and (c) it provides us a definition that opens expertise up to more people. Very few of us have a shot at winning an Olympic medal. But almost all of us can progressively advance on the problems of leading in education.

Leading in education is complex, changeable, and frustrating. Expertise in that role is not about stellar performance before an admiring audience but about recognizing and dealing effectively with the problems of school leadership and then doing that again the next day and the next month and yet again when the problems morph into different ones. The payoff is not in winning fame or fortune but in making better the lives of children, school faculties and staffs, and communities.

QUESTION 4: HOW MIGHT WE THINK ABOUT THE PLACE OF TECHNOLOGY IN EDUCATION?

What might technology do for our leadership of education as we advance on the problems of practice? Notice that our question is not, "Is technology *impressive?*" There are certainly whiz-bang mind-blowing phenomena in technology that we could not imagine in our childhood. Some of those phenomena could not even be imagined by computer experts just a few decades ago.

Since then, technology has permeated practically all aspects of our lives. But our question is not how impressed we should be with technology but how likely it is to help us as leaders pursue our ideals for education, how likely it is to help us, over the course of our careers, progressively advance on the problems of practice. Your answer to that question depends on assumptions you make about it.

Strobel and Tillberg-Webb (2009) identified four assumptions educators might hold about technologies. The first two are interpretations of technology's *place in social change* and the last two are attempts to predict *the future that social change will bring*. The four assumptions are as follows: (a) technological determinism, (b) social determinism, (c) technological utopianism, and (d) technological dystopianism.

Assumptions *a* and *b* are about the causes of social change. People who assume *technological* determinism believe technology is "the fundamental force of social change" and that technology's development and progress moves "according to its own internal logic" (Strobel & Tillberg-Webb, 2009, p. 77). In this view, human perspectives on how we ought to use technology seem of relatively minor importance. However, people who assume *social* determinism believe many processes—"social, political, cultural, and economic" (p. 78)—influence social change and that these processes drive the development and use of technology.

Assumptions *c* and *d* are about the future that technology will bring. Those who assume technological *utopianism* emphasize "societal benefits to technological tool use" (Strobel & Tillberg-Webb, 2009, p. 79): improved ability to access and analyze information and thus better decision making, more efficiency and effectiveness, and improved lives for most of us. On the other hand, those who assume technological *dystopianism* are wary that technologies will permeate all aspects of human life and make the lives of most of us less free, less meaningful, and less just.

Webster (2017) found among PK–12 technology leaders an additional, more down-to-earth assumption: "Technology is nothing more than a tool" (2017, p. 27). Webster wrote that this assumption is consistent with a more formally stated view, "*Educational goals and curriculum should drive technology*" (p. 27, emphasis original). But he also found technology leaders to assume technological determinism, the view that "technology is always changing and you must change with it or you will be left behind" (p. 30).

Before we leave these perspectives, we emphasize that your beliefs can fall along the continuum of these four perspectives; you can hold combinations of these four perspectives; and you can even believe ideas that seem to be in tension with one another, such as technological determinism (we cannot control the kinds or the rates of changes) and technological utopianism (technology will provide all of us with more freedom and fulfillment).

Webster (2017) documented that technology leaders tended to have two views that seemed to be in tension with one another: (a) *"Educational goals and curriculum should drive technology"* and (b) *"Keep up with technology (or be left behind)"* (p. 29, emphasis original). Webster explained that leaders may believe both that educational goals and curriculum should drive technology, and that technology is so all-pervasive in today's society that leading students to become conversant with those technologies should be an education goal and part of the curriculum.

We understand how education leaders can feel at the mercy of seemingly irresistible forces. Both social forces and technological developments can seem to stifle our initiatives. But we cannot see how we can simultaneously call ourselves education leaders and totally buy into determinism. As leaders, our call is to resist, change, or at least ameliorate forces that inhibit the capacities of school systems to serve "all children and youth, providing them with richly engaging, challenging, and supported opportunities to learn" (Education Deans for Justice and Equity & National Education Policy Center, 2017, p. 2).

This resistance, changing, and amelioration is by no means easy, but we can grow in expertise to progressively advance on the problems of education. The chapters that follow, from educators passionately devoted to their practice, can help us grow in that expertise.

OVERVIEW OF THE BOOK

Leaders need to make good decisions, and information can inform our decision making. The more we know and understand, the better our decisions should be. In chapter 1, Kevin Badgett explains how the wonderful convenience of the iPad can be put in service to finding information where and when we need it. He describes how we can search for research literature or any other documents relevant to problems a school leader might face.

Leaders also need to monitor what is going on in our organizations, find out what people are thinking, make sense of it, and use that sense to guide our decisions. Chad R. Lochmiller and Jessica N. Lester describe ways education leaders can base decisions on qualitative data, moving us beyond the quantitative data that accountability systems have pushed us to consider. In chapter 2, they introduce software both for iPads and for desktop computers that will help us analyze qualitative data to enhance our understanding of situations we face.

For chapter 3, Sharon Wilbur, Sharon Dean, Leslie Williams, Linda Atkinson, and Jean Cate provide a compelling discussion of classroom walkthroughs. If the school accomplishes its goals largely through its teachers, then we should be familiar with what those teachers are doing, where their work should be celebrated, and where it may need tweaking. But often the time principals spend in walkthroughs is not well used. Wilbur et al. focus not merely on getting walkthroughs done but on attending to our purpose in doing them. They describe software for the iPad that keeps us focused on the purpose of the walkthrough and helps store, organize, and analyze the findings from walkthroughs.

We leaders must be masterful communicators. This is especially true for superintendents, who must attend to and respond to communications from inside and outside their districts. At the same time, we must be creating our own messages and sharing them widely. Superintendent John Tienhaara, David Wicks, and Thomas Alsbury invite us in chapter 4 to consider communication in school leadership. They describe ways we may use Internet applications to enhance our communication with our various communities.

As school leaders progressively advance on the problems we face, we need support for our own learning, both in terms of better ideas and sometimes in terms of emotional boosts from colleagues. In chapter 5, Julia L. Parra describes how we can use technology to support the pursuit of expertise. Her chapter enhances our understanding of how to search for information, directs us in networking with others for guidance and mutual support, and helps us deal with the need to curate, that is, to keep track of all the information and contacts we gain through social media.

We hope if you are reading our book that you are an administrator or someone who is interested in administration. If either of those conditions is true, you need to be concerned about legal issues. So we are pleased to offer, in chapter 6, advice from Robert F. Hachiya on dealing with those legal issues. We conclude the book with a glossary to clarify some terms tossed around by the more technology-oriented among us.

We reiterate that if you are a principal or other school leader, you are doing some of the most important and commendable work of our society. You have our utmost admiration for taking on this education role. We hope our book makes a helpful contribution to your efforts.

REFERENCES

Bereiter, C., & Scardamalia, M. (1993). *Surpassing ourselves: An inquiry into the nature and implications of expertise*. Chicago, IL: Open Court.

Education Deans for Justice and Equity & National Education Policy Center. (2017, January). *Public education, democracy, and the role of the federal government: A declaration of principles.* Retrieved from National Education Policy Center website: http://nepc.colorado.edu/files/publications/Deans%20Letter1.17.17.pdf

Seashore Louis, K. S., Leithwood, K., Wahlstrom, K. L., & Anderson, S. E. (2010). *Learning from leadership: Investigating the links to improved student learning.* Retrieved from Wallace Foundation website: http://www.wallacefoundation.org/knowledge-center/Documents/Investigating-the-Links-to-Improved-Student-Learning.pdf

Skrla, L., McKenzie, K. B., & Scheurich, J. J. (2009). *Using equity audits to create equitable and excellent schools.* Thousand Oaks, CA: Corwin Press.

Strobel, J., & Tillberg-Webb, H. (2009). Applying a critical and humanizing framework of instructional technologies to educational practice. In L. Moller, J. B. Huett, & D. M. Harvey (Eds.), *Learning and instructional technologies for the 21st century: Visions of the future* (pp. 75–93). New York, NY: Springer.

Webster, M. D. (2017). Philosophy of technology assumptions in educational technology leadership. *Educational Technology & Society, 20*(1), 25–36.

Acknowledgments

When Rowman & Littlefield Education invited us to do this book, we asked contacts around the United States to suggest how technology could help school leaders do our jobs and get better at doing them. Our contacts introduced us to their contacts, and all of these people gave us great suggestions for our book design. We then invited educators around the United States to submit proposals for chapters, and we had other educators review these proposals and give us feedback and suggestions. Finally, we invited selected people to write chapters for the book.

We are very pleased with their work. We express our gratitude and appreciation to John Nash, of the University of Kentucky, for his ideas and support in the design of this book, and to three experts who reviewed an earlier version of this manuscript: Julia Ballenger, of Texas A&M University, Commerce; Teena MacDonald, of Washington State University; and Tom Koerner, of Rowman & Littlefield Education.

We especially thank the authors for their enthusiasm in sharing their knowledge and inspiration and their patience as we labored to synthesize their valuable contributions into a coherent work. We list authors and reviewers at the end of this book. Finally, we thank Maria Cristina Padilla for her editing and formatting work on the final manuscript and for her excellent contributions to the glossary.

Chapter One

The Right Information When You Need It

The iPad and iBooks

Kevin Badgett

KEY POINTS IN THIS CHAPTER

- Leaders are responsible for providing timely information to others in their schools.
- The iPad application, iBooks, can facilitate locating pertinent information.
- Despite its name, iBooks allows storage and retrieval of all kinds of documents, not just books. This can include laws, regulations, and board policies.
- You can often keep and share in iBooks peer-reviewed articles and books on best practices, even without a journal subscription or a library membership.

TECHNOLOGY AND SCHOOL LEADERSHIP: EFFICIENCY TOOLS

Given the immensely broad and diverse roles and responsibilities of the principalship, it is important to identify and use tools that support our ability to coordinate human, material, fiscal, and time resources in a way that supports the improvement of teaching and learning. As efficiency tools, technological innovations come with many benefits.

OVERCOMING OUR RESISTANCE TO TECHNOLOGY

Practicing school leaders know teachers often lack enthusiasm when asked to integrate innovative technology into their everyday practice. This is true throughout the history of American education. According to Ryan and Cooper (2013), early 19th-century teachers expressed anxiety and reluctance to incorporate the use of a brand-new tool into their instruction. They were trained and tutored, given manuals and coached; yet they were still reluctant. That new technology: the chalkboard.

Technologies today also present challenges and evoke anxiety in teachers (Ribeiro, 2014). In fact, school leaders frequently interact with technology with the same fears. Waxman, Boriack, Lee, and MacNeil (2013) suggest many administrators are novices when it comes to the use of technology.

But if we are going to ensure the education children receive is relevant and responsive to the world for which we are preparing them, we must use the technologies that will enhance our leadership competencies. Furthermore, when principals have positive attitudes about technologies, teachers tend to accept the importance of technology in the classroom (Waxman et al., 2013).

RESEARCH AND TOOLS: IBOOKS

To make decisions, teachers and leaders often need information. In the hectic rush of leading a school, it is reasonable to expect administrators will sometimes neglect to follow through on a promise to get requested information to teachers. If that happens too frequently, however, administrators can lose credibility and even teachers' support.

Conversely, experienced school leaders know teachers appreciate accurate information delivered quickly. Effective use of the Internet capabilities of the iPad can support the administrator's ability to find answers to teachers' questions.

Teachers may need information on best practices, campus or district policies, or law and policy. With an iPad in hand, administrators can often point teachers immediately to a helpful source rather than just promising to "get back to" the teacher in the future.

One valuable application (app) available on the iPad is iBooks. iBooks may already be preloaded on your iPad. If it is not, you can download it to your iPad from the App Store. If there's not already an app for the App Store on your iPad, you can use a search engine to find it.

With iBooks, a leader can develop a repository of searchable documents to facilitate communication of information. iBooks is also helpful because, in addition to a repository of resources, it supplies the user with a range of tools that increases administrators' efficiency, thereby freeing them to effectively handle other day-to-day challenges. Figure 1.1 shows the iBooks app on an iPad.

To save a document to iBooks, one must open a PDF document on the iPad. After opening the document, the user should select the option to "Open in iBooks" in the top right-hand corner of the document under the website address bar (figure 1.2).

As figure 1.3 shows, the uploaded document is now at home in the iBooks application. It is the third document in the figure.

Figure 1.1. The iBooks App

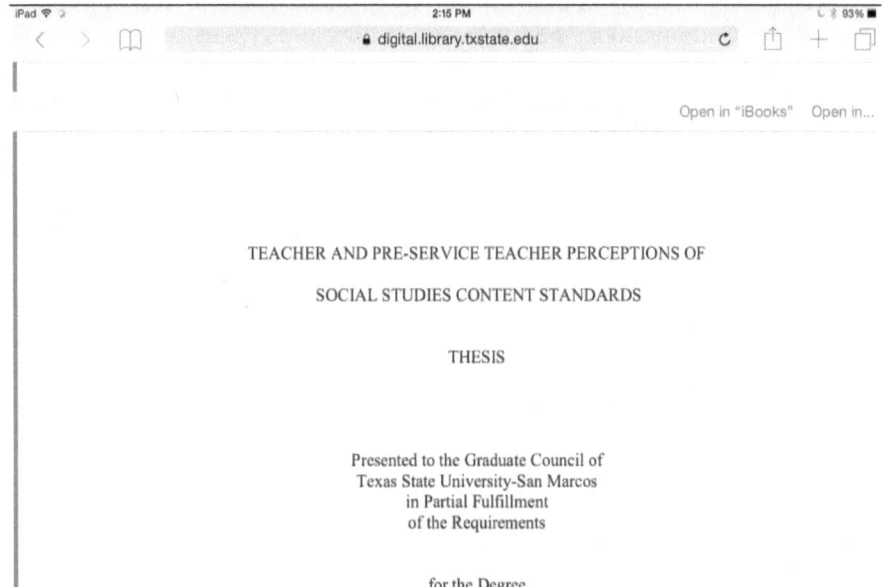

Figure 1.2. Save a Document to iBooks

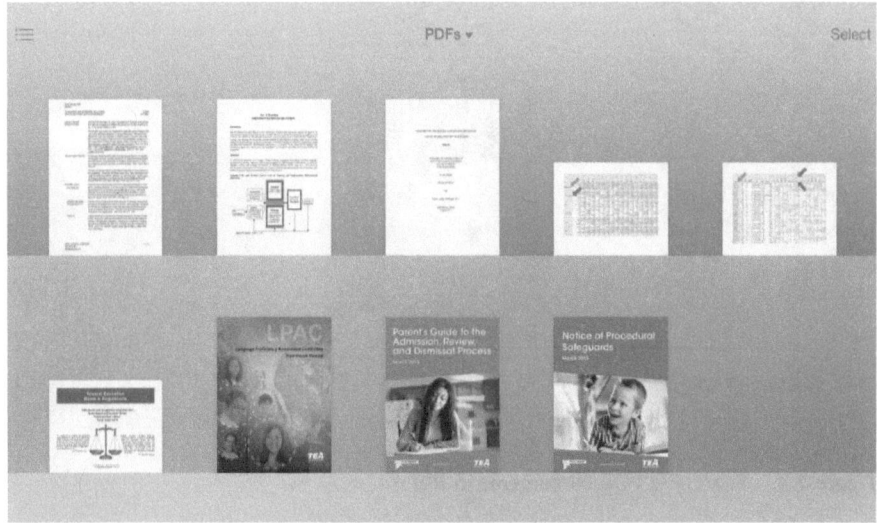

Figure 1.3. Uploaded Documents Saved to iBooks Home Page

DECISIONS INFORMED BY REGULATIONS

You should consider including several kinds of documents in iBooks. One kind is regulatory. For example, in Texas there is a document for special educators accessible via a link to The Legal Framework found on the Region 18 Education Service Center website (TEA, 2016). The Special Education Rules and Regulations document offers a side-by-side alignment of federal regulations, Texas Commissioner's/State Board of Education Rules, and Texas state laws. Stored in iBooks, this document can be at the school leader's fingertips.

PDF documents are also searchable in iBooks. Figure 1.4 shows a manual for a Language Proficiency Assessment Committee (LPAC). We can use iBooks to search such a manual. Once you tap on the magnifying glass icon and type the relevant text, a menu of options will emerge (under the magnifying glass icon). From there, you can select the desired reference, and iBooks will take you directly to the relevant text.

School board policy documents are no longer only available in giant dusty tomes hidden at the back of a shelf in the principal's office. Rather, saved in PDF form and uploaded to iBooks (see the first document in the iBooks home screenshot in figure 1.3), board policy can inform operational decisions as intended (figure 1.5).

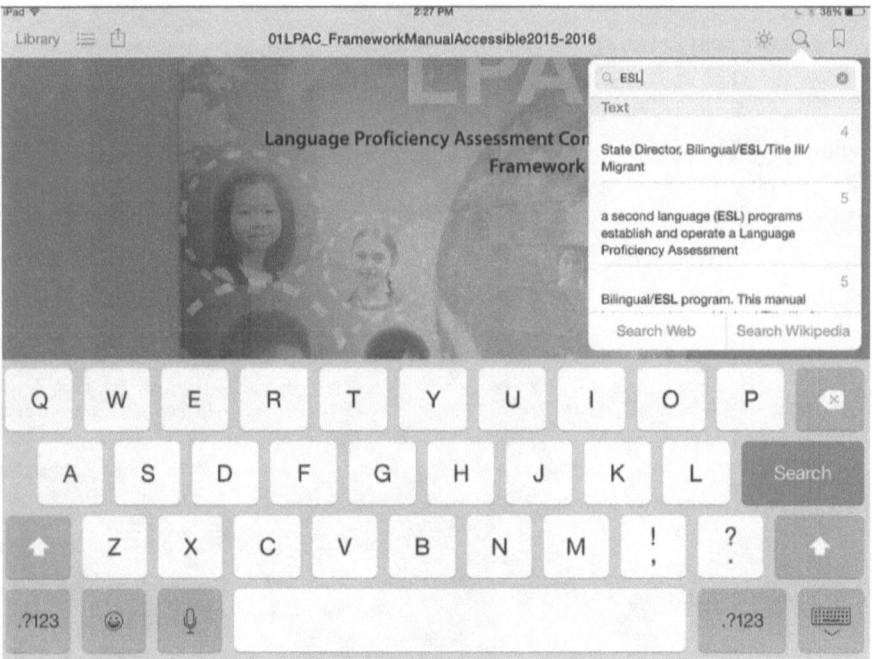

Figure 1.4. Searching PDF Documents in iBooks

The Right Information When You Need It

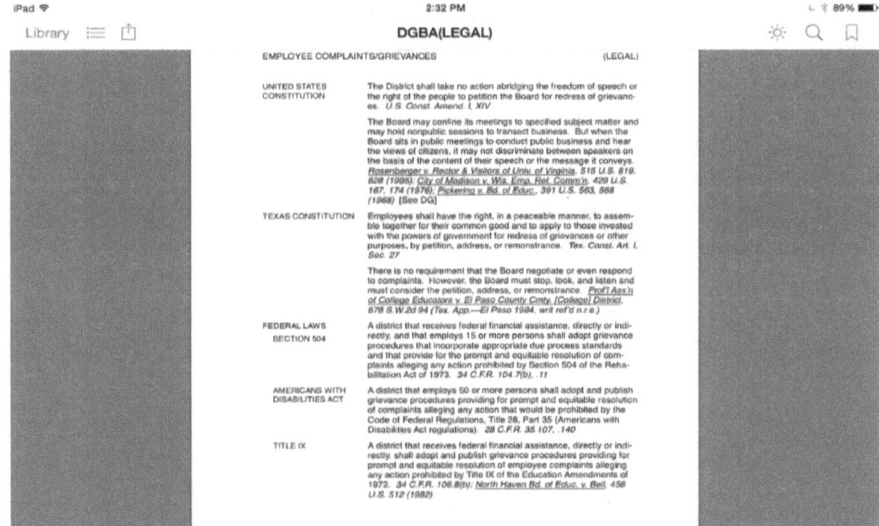

Figure 1.5. School Board Policy Document

With databases such as Google Scholar, you can often find peer-reviewed articles and books on best practices, even without a journal subscription or a library membership. You can share these articles and books with a teacher looking for ideas by attaching a document from iBooks to an email and sending a quick note with a page reference.

To email a document from iBooks, you simply tap on the Upload icon, which is close to the top left-hand corner of the screen near the word "Library" and select the "Email" option in the drop-down menu (figure 1.6).

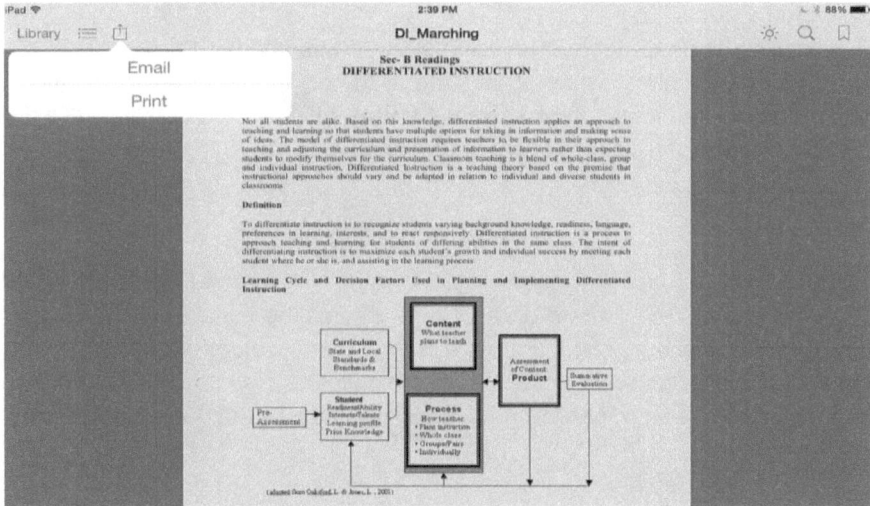

Figure 1.6. Emailing a Document From iBooks

When helping teachers address needs in the classroom, you might often find answers to their questions in documents that you can save in iBooks and access later. You can meet with teachers and share information in passing conversations while you are in the halls during class changes.

Today's school leaders need to be equipped with tools that support the timely acquisition and communication of information. With tools like iBooks and the mobile Internet access allowed by the iPad, school leaders can be much more responsive with data and information than those who choose not to take advantage of such tools.

For more insights on this topic, read Julia Parra's chapter on searching, curating, and networking in this book.

CAUTIONS

There are limitations to consider when using this technology. First, there is a danger that the iPad, like any technology, could become a gimmick. Without training that supports an integrated use of the iPad, you could make the iPad a mere "bell and whistle" that adds little to your effectiveness.

Besides initial training on the iPad, it is important that you receive some degree of ongoing support and mentoring. Failure to support administrators using this or any new technology can compromise procedural fidelity and, ultimately, hurt the overall effective execution of basic leadership responsibilities.

Second, introducing the iPad while implementing other technological initiatives and innovations risks overwhelming those who are learning to use the technology amid their everyday responsibilities. As valuable as this tool is, if a district has a greater priority in the moment, it may be a good idea to delay the introduction of the iPad.

Bringing the iPad in while focusing attention on another initiative will not only limit the practical value of the iPad in the beginning of an implementation effort but can also compromise the ability of school leaders to grasp the benefits of this tool for the school leader and teachers.

CONCLUSION

Ultimately, everything done on a campus should be considered in light of how it affects teaching and learning. It is vital that we identify and implement tools that help increase the leader's effectiveness as it relates to teaching and learning. But it is important to remember, as I noted at the beginning of this chapter, that the introduction of a new initiative is often met with skepticism and anxiety by teachers and administrators alike.

By providing initial training and follow-up support, the principal (or district, depending on the source of the initiative) can effectively introduce and fully integrate this helpful tool into the everyday normal management processes and thereby support a school's ability to ensure student success.

REFERENCES

Ribeiro, J. (2014). Teacher technology adoption and the philosophy of fear. *Antistasis*, *4*(2). Retrieved from https://journals.lib.unb.ca/index.php/antistasis/article/view/22310/25909

Ryan, K., & Cooper, J. (2013). *Those who can, teach* (13th ed.). Belmont, CA: Cengage Learning.

TEA. (2016). *Special education rules and regulations.* Retrieved from https://framework.esc18.net/Documents/Side_by_Side.pdf

Waxman, H. C., Boriack, A. W., Lee, Y. H., & MacNeil, A. (2013). Principals' perceptions of the importance of technology in schools. *Contemporary Educational Technology*, *4*(3), 187–196.

Chapter Two

The Qualitative Side of Data-Driven Leadership

Using Computer-Assisted Qualitative Data Analysis Software to Inform and Guide Leadership Practice

Chad R. Lochmiller & Jessica N. Lester

KEY POINTS IN THIS CHAPTER

- Data-driven decision-making is often informed by *quantitative* evidence. But *qualitative* evidence can provide meaningful guidance for school leaders.
- Educational leaders can analyze qualitative data to make sense of people's perspectives and experiences.
- There is software available to facilitate analyses of qualitative evidence. We focus here on ATLAS.ti for the iPad, a free application.
- Qualitative inquiry is notorious for the amount and variety of data involved. But using ATLAS.ti software to analyze qualitative data makes it easier to handle.
- We explain briefly how ATLAS.ti works and provide practical examples of topics educational leaders might want to investigate with ATLAS.ti.

School and district leaders face increasing calls to use various types of data to inform their leadership practice (Coburn & Turner, 2011). Within the broader educational leadership literature, there exists a variety of leadership models of data-driven decision-making (e.g., Bauer & Brazer, 2012; Boudett, City, & Murnane, 2014; Goldring & Berends, 2009). Much discussion about data-driven decision-making has cast it as relying mostly on data from student learning assessments and standardized tests (Wayman, Spring, Lemke, & Lehr, 2012).

While these numeric data points have been widely used to inform leadership practice and teaching practice, we should not forget qualitative data (texts, pictures, or other artifacts, e.g., student work samples, parent questionnaires, teacher meeting notes, and planning documents). These can provide valuable insights about the perspectives of key school stakeholders as well as firsthand evidence of student learning. As such, qualitative data can provide meaningful guidance for school leaders.

Despite the availability of qualitative data, much of the literature about data-driven decision-making has neglected how qualitative information can inform practice to assist leaders in addressing student learning needs. Rather, many leaders and most data-driven decision-making courses and texts focus almost entirely on student assessments and other quantitative data.

One possible reason for this focus is that the tools available to leaders to access, organize, make sense of, and report about qualitative data are not well known within the educational leadership literature. Indeed, most of the discussions about tools that can be used to perform qualitative data analysis reside within the broader qualitative research methods literature.

So in this chapter we highlight how leaders might use computer-assisted qualitative data analysis software (CAQDAS), e.g., Dedoose, ATLAS.ti, MAXQDA, NVivo, and others as part of their data-driven leadership practice. We focus specifically on ATLAS.ti for the iPad, given that the software (specifically the iPad version) is currently a free download from the Apple App Store. We note, however, that any CAQDAS package can be used to support qualitative data analysis. Further, CAQDAS desktop software packages—which ATLAS.ti provides—might be useful as well.

In this chapter, we consider the qualitative side of data-driven leadership, noting how qualitative data can inform educational leaders' thinking. Next, we describe the essential features of ATLAS.ti for the iPad, particularly those helpful to educational leaders seeking to use ATLAS.ti as part of their regular leadership practice. Finally, we conclude with some short vignettes to show how leaders might use ATLAS.ti for the iPad in their leadership practice.

UNDERSTANDING THE QUALITATIVE SIDE OF DATA-DRIVEN LEADERSHIP

An assumption in data-driven leadership is that leaders can use systematically collected data to inform their leadership practice. Data-driven leadership assumes that leaders engage in "in-depth data analysis focused on student learning" and that this "will be a routine part of teachers' and administrators' daily work" (Knapp, Copland, Swinnerton, & Monpas-Huber, 2006, p. 3). As such, educational leaders use data to become more specific and thoughtful about the leadership actions they take—focusing primarily on classrooms and challenges associated with teaching and learning (Anderson, Leithwood, & Strauss, 2010).

Surprisingly, only within the past decade do we find increasing attention in the research literature to how educational leaders identify data sources to inform their decisions and interpret these sources of data and what they do in response (Ikemoto & Marsh, 2007; Kerr, Marsh, Ikemoto, Darilek, & Barney, 2006; Luo, 2008; Marsh, Pane, & Hamilton, 2006). We add here our perspectives about (a) the ways in which data can be used to support practice and (b) new and potentially useful tools.

Historically, writers have framed data-driven decision-making in terms of using student assessment results to inform practice (Marsh et al., 2006; Wayman et al., 2012; Wayman & Stringfield, 2006; Young, 2006; Ysseldyke & Tardew, 2007). This may reflect the realities of the current accountability environment, which has prioritized state tests and other student assessments as the primary type of evidence to use (Roderick, 2012). Yet this vastly oversimplifies the types of information available to leaders to make informed decisions about educational improvement. Indeed, Goldring and Berends (2009) noted:

> Data refer to multiple sources and types of information. Although many think of scores on standardized tests as the main type of data, other data include information about the students, school programs, and other measures of student learning such as student work, ongoing formative assessments, and portfolios. Data are not limited to students and programs. Data include observations of the quality of teaching and content of the curriculum actually taught in the classroom. (p. 15)

Such a conception broadens our view of what data educational leaders might use to inform their practice but also raises new challenges. For example, qualitative data can be challenging to collect, store, analyze, and then access. Unlike numeric data that are stored in increasingly robust information systems and thus are available to leaders with relative ease (Wayman et al., 2012), qualitative information is often found in disconnected, incompatible forms that make analyzing this information difficult.

Generally speaking, educational leaders analyze qualitative data to make sense of an individual's perspectives and experiences within the context of a classroom, school, program, district, or event (Denzin & Lincoln, 2005; Polkinghorne, 2005). Yet without tools to engage in this analysis, such information often sits idle and is thus not widely used to inform practice, shape local understanding of educational challenges, or monitor the impact and implementation of educational interventions.

QUALITATIVE DATA SOURCES AND THE QUALITATIVE DATA ANALYSIS PROCESS

In schools and districts, qualitative data may be readily available (e.g., teachers' lesson plans). Or you may need to collect it for a specific purpose, for example, by interviewing or conducting focus groups with parents or students. In each of these cases, the data are qualitative, that is, they are not numbers but are spoken or written language (Polkinghorne, 2005). Table 2.1 provides a summary by organizational level of some of the common qualitative data sources available to school leaders, which they can use to inform their decision-making or leadership practice. This list is merely illustrative, not exhaustive.

Table 2.1. Examples of Qualitative Data

Student/Classroom	School	District/Community
• Assignments	• Department meeting notes	• Accountability reports
• Assessments/exams	• Open house feedback forms	• Budget narratives
• Classroom talk/conversation	• Parent communications	• Community newsletters
• Individualized education plan	• Parent questionnaires	• Community questionnaires
• Lesson plans	• Professional Learning Community documents	• District improvement plans
• Parent communications	• School communications	• School board meeting notes
• Student work	• School improvement plan	• Strategic planning documents
	• Student discipline reports	
	• Teacher observation notes	

Given the breadth of qualitative data available to school and district leaders, it is not surprising that such information is difficult for educational leaders to analyze. As Bauer and Brazer (2012) noted, collecting and analyzing qualitative data "requires more effort [than does quantitative data] because it comes from talking to people, observing in classrooms, and examining documents" (p. 11). To put this in practical terms, an educational leader who takes notes during 30-minute conversations with all of the classroom teachers at the beginning of the school year might have many pages of data to analyze.

Likewise, educational leaders who review classroom instruction might find themselves drowning in notebooks or legal pads, should they not use their laptop or Apple iPad to record information obtained during classroom observations. In each case, the value of qualitative data can be outweighed by how cumbersome it is. Thus finding tools for qualitative data analysis is essential if educational leaders are to access and assess this valuable information. We highlight one tool in this chapter.

Analyzing Qualitative Data

Analyzing qualitative data requires skill. While it is beyond the scope of this chapter to describe qualitative analysis thoroughly, we provide a shortened description. For further reading, we encourage you to review descriptions in the existing literature about the qualitative data analysis process (e.g., Lochmiller & Lester, 2017; Miles, Huberman, & Saldaña, 2014). We provide below a condensed version of the qualitative analysis process as you would use it for ATLAS.ti on the iPad.

Qualitative analysis relies on educational leaders' abilities to determine what the information's relevance might be for the particular questions or challenges they have. Qualitative analysis requires leaders to attach meaning to the material they are reading. Thus leaders must draw on their own experience to make sense of the information. In addition, it is important to keep in mind that qualitative analysis often occurs alongside the data collection process. In other words, as you collect data, you also begin to analyze it. As you analyze the data, you begin to become aware of what additional data might be needed to answer your questions.

Qualitative analysis often results in the production of "themes" or broad statements about the data that highlight central ideas. This approach might be called "thematic analysis." The themes are generated through coding. That is, we use codes to attach an interpretation to a specific passage of text (Saldaña, 2009). Codes are short labels that signify what the passage of text is about.

After applying codes, the leader combines codes, noting relationships between and across the various passages of the data. Eventually, the leader can group these codes into categories that capture more general ideas noted in the data. Similarly, categories can be further grouped into themes. So we are moving from codes to categories to themes.

Computer-Assisted Qualitative-Data-Analysis Software (CAQDAS)

CAQDAS software has been used to facilitate qualitative research (Paulus, Lester, & Dempster, 2014). CAQDAS software packages tend to consist of a database for storing qualitative data, a mechanism for coding text, a query tool with which you can retrieve highlighted passages of text, and a memo or note-taking function that allows you to document your impressions about the data you are reviewing. The purpose of the software is not to perform the analysis for you but rather to assist in completing the analysis in a more efficient and (at times) robust manner.

There are a number of software packages available, including ATLAS.ti, Dedoose, MAXQDA, and NVivo. In this chapter, we highlight ATLAS.ti for the iPad as it is currently a free download through the Apple App Store and offers educational leaders the functionality of a CAQDAS package without the complexity of a full research suite. However, as noted previously, most CAQDAS packages can be used for analyses to support educational leadership practice.

ATLAS.TI FOR THE IPAD: A SUPPORTIVE TECHNOLOGY TOOL FOR EDUCATIONAL LEADERS

ATLAS.ti for the iPad is based on the larger ATLAS.ti desktop software package. The desktop version includes more robust analytic features and can perform a wider array of research tasks. However, the desktop version lacks portability and thus may be difficult for educational leaders to use in their daily practice.

The iPad version is smaller but allows educational leaders to create "project files" wherein documents and other qualitative evidence can be stored, analyzed, and later retrieved. ATLAS.ti for the iPad allows leaders to import documents in a variety of electronic formats, which includes importing files as audio and video clips, image files, PDF files, and files in Microsoft Office formats. Leaders can also import information from a linked Dropbox account. Such features ensure that educational leaders are able to retrieve and store information on the go.

Figure 2.1 shows the opening screen in ATLAS.ti for the iPad and depicts a typical project. As the screenshot illustrates, the document screen provides users with convenient access to new documents and data sources drawn both from internal storage on their iPad or, as illustrated, from a cloud-based storage system such as Dropbox.

ATLAS.ti for the iPad has common terminology with the desktop application. *Project files* refers to the primary file wherein a leader stores data, performs analysis, and includes notes. *Documents* refers to the data that is stored within the project file. Documents can take a number of different forms and can be either retrieved from a cloud storage platform (e.g., Dropbox) or created using the iPad's camera and microphone. *Quotations* refers to sections of text, audio clips, or video clips that are selected by the educational leader as being important or relevant to the questions being raised.

Codes, as noted above, are applied to quotations and are intended to attach a particular meaning to the passage of text. Saldaña (2009) defined a code as "a word or short phrase that symbolically assigns a summative, salient, essence-capturing, and/or evocative attribute for a portion of language-based or visual data" (p. 3). Codes can be created *before* an educational leader reads

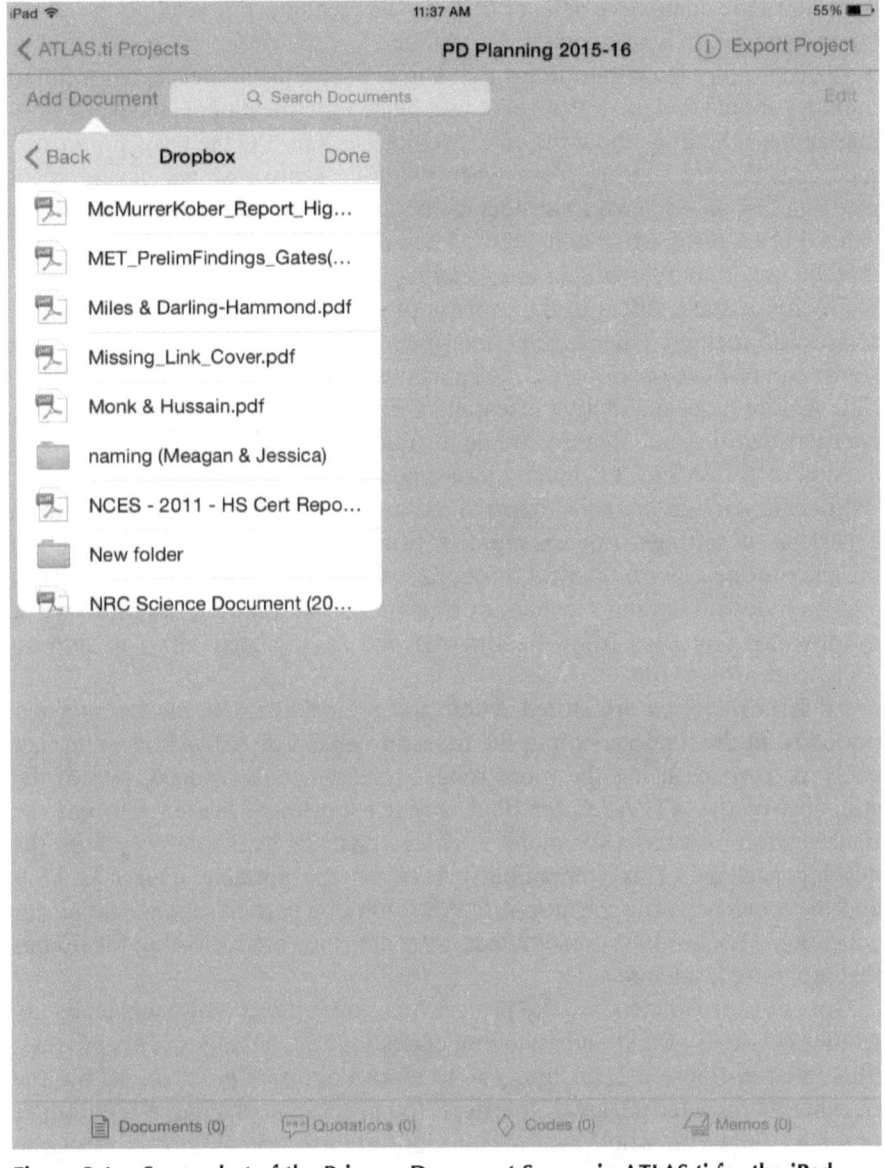

Figure 2.1. Screenshot of the Primary Document Screen in ATLAS.ti for the iPad

or reviews the qualitative data, or they can be created *while* reading the qualitative material, in a more emergent fashion.

Memos refers to written notes that capture an educational leader's initial thinking about the data or that serve as a place for educational leaders to summarize their thinking about the data. Memos can serve as the basis for written reports, a helpful starting place when planning a professional development presentation, or as a working document that can be later exported and expanded upon using Microsoft Word. They can even themselves become data that the qualitative researcher later analyzes.

Finally, a *query* refers to the process of retrieving coded passages of text or specific memos. Queries function much like an Internet search in that a leader can retrieve previously coded portions of text using the query function. This feature helps qualitative researchers find the passages that support their codes, categories, and themes. While the query function is limited in the iPad version of ATLAS.ti, it is much more robust on the desktop version.

Educational leaders can import files into their ATLAS.ti project file in a variety of settings. For example, a principal might gather information during routine classroom walkthroughs, as part of a data collection effort that includes classroom teachers or a professional learning community, or by downloading files from the Internet and saving them directly into an ATLAS.ti project file.

All files imported are stored within the project file and can be later exported from the iPad version to the desktop version of ATLAS.ti for further analysis, perhaps using the more robust research tools. Indeed, one of the strengths of the ATLAS.ti for iPad is that educational leaders can use the iPad version as a basis for more extensive analysis available only with the desktop package. This compatibility between the portable iPad ATLAS.ti and the more powerful desktop ATLAS.ti may be particularly appealing for educational leaders who contemplate using data they are collecting for studies that are more academic.

Once data are loaded into the project file, you interact with the data by selecting passages of text and attaching codes to these passages. This process, illustrated in figure 2.2, enables you to mark important passages within the documents for later retrieval. In effect, the process works like a highlighter or sticky note you would use to note important statements or passages in paper documents.

But where coding in Atlas.ti is better than the highlighter or the sticky note is that it permits you to query the information and retrieve specific passages. In other words, if you marked a number of passages with the code, "reading for main idea," you could later do a search of all documents for the code

The Qualitative Side of Data-Driven Leadership 17

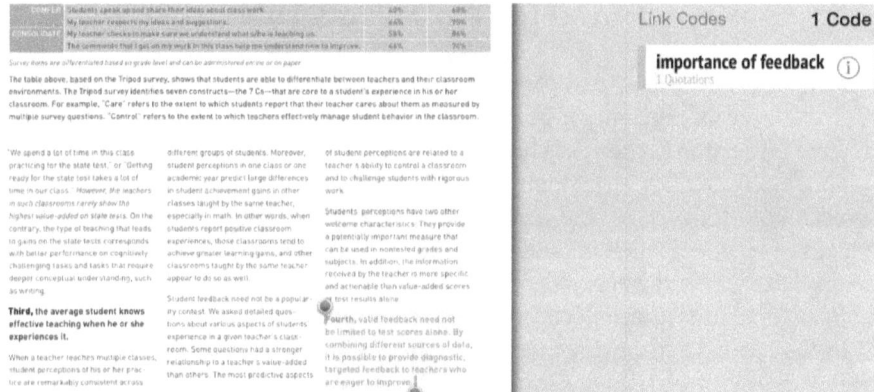

Figure 2.2. Selecting a Passage of Text and Coding It

"reading for main idea," and retrieve in one batch all the ones you had coded with "reading for main idea."

It can be useful to attach memos (or notes) to passages of text you code. Attaching memos enables you to document your initial interpretations, hunches, or questions about your data. You record these insights for later consideration or use. For example, you might code a passage regarding a particular strategy and also attach a memo that captures your interpretation of the information and how you intend to use the information in practice. In figure 2.3, an educational leader reviewing a report about giving teachers feedback uses a memo to record points that might later be discussed in a faculty meeting.

These memos can also serve as an outline for a written report or as a running record that captures the educational leader's evolving interpretations. Such a record may be especially valuable when data analysis is carried out as part of a professional learning community, grade level team, or leadership team within which participants might offer varying interpretations, perspectives, or ideas.

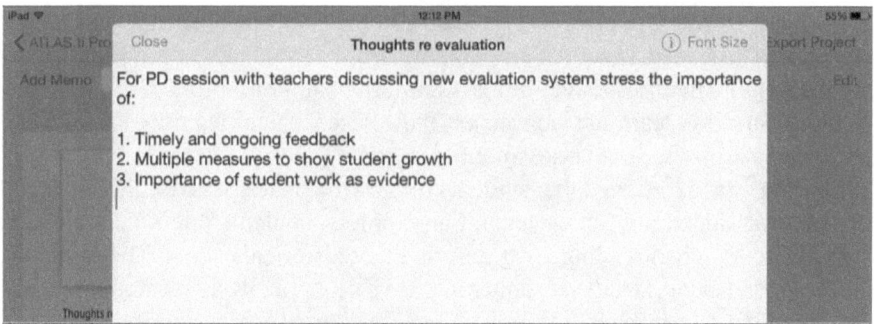

Figure 2.3. Recording Points in a Memo

EXAMPLES FROM PRACTICE

Having reviewed the basic features of ATLAS.ti, we will illustrate how ATLAS.ti for the iPad might be used to support data-driven leadership practice in three leadership scenarios. These scenarios illustrate how educational leaders might employ ATLAS.ti in their practice. In the first scenario, we focus on the principal of Stoneybrook Elementary. In this scenario, the principal works with a team of teacher leaders to analyze student work. We see how ATLAS.ti can be used to support the analysis of documents retrieved from classrooms as well as its potential to inform decisions about classroom instruction.

In the second scenario, we focus on an instructional coach at Westminster Middle School who uses the software to record videos of classroom instruction and then share best practices with colleagues in the school. We highlight how the coach might use the iPad and software technology to help teachers consider new instructional behaviors that support higher levels of student engagement.

In the third scenario, we highlight efforts by a central office administrator in the Hillsdale School District to improve district support for principals. The central office administrator draws upon open-ended survey responses to inform decisions about how her department could improve its support. In this scenario, we show how leaders can draw upon data from other technology tools (e.g., SurveyMonkey) to submit to the analytic power of ATLAS.ti. In each of these cases, ATLAS.ti for the iPad helps leaders understand key issues in the school and district—none of which are directly informed by quantitative student assessment data.

Analyzing Student Work at Stoneybrook Elementary

Stoneybrook Elementary School is located in the Hillsdale School District and serves an urban community. It enrolls 650 students in kindergarten through eighth grade. The principal and a team of classroom teachers lead the school's improvement efforts. The team has recently engaged in an extensive analysis of student test scores and determined that students in the sixth grade are having difficulties developing summaries of nonfiction readings. The principal and his team are concerned that these difficulties may affect their performance on the state assessment.

Teachers have observed that students often struggle to prepare coherent summaries of assigned nonfiction texts. For example, students often incompletely summarize assigned readings that describe key historical events. The principal and teacher leaders decide to undertake a yearlong analysis of student work. The principal asks teachers to begin collecting examples of writing assignments in which students summarize nonfiction texts. The principal asks the teachers to upload PDFs of the writing assignments to a shared Dropbox folder.

In all, the teachers collect examples from three assigned nonfiction texts and submit more than 250 pages of student work samples from students who struggled to summarize the assigned nonfiction reading. With such an immense data set, the principal quickly feels overwhelmed by the amount of information he needs to sift through. Recognizing that analyzing student work might reveal important details, though, he decides to adopt ATLAS.ti for the iPad to support his analysis.

The principal begins his analysis by loading the documents into an ATLAS.ti project file. He hopes that using ATLAS.ti will allow him to more easily highlight and retrieve passages from the student work samples to share with teachers during professional development sessions. His primary goal is to attempt to quantify the information by coding passages of text and then calculating their frequencies to show teachers what problems occur most often.

The principal begins by highlighting passages within the samples of work where students have omitted important details. As the principal reviews an increasing number of student work samples he notes that he is consistently highlighting passages of text where students needed to interpret the author's meaning. At this point, he realizes it would be useful to involve the teachers in coding the data as well, thereby creating an opportunity to dialogue about the instructional practices. Thus, he begins by meeting with three to four teachers and together they code the data.

Probing further, they find that students are also failing to identify the most important facts in the nonfiction readings. Instead of reporting only significant events, actions, or factual statements, the students report minor details that are not essential to the summary. Armed with this understanding, the principal and teachers continue coding across the student work sample. After completing the reading and coding, they generate the frequencies of codes that they attached to the highlighted passages across the student work.

They find that nearly 75 percent of the codes that were applied to the samples were related in some way to "interpretation" or "distinguishing between important and unimportant statements." After completing the analysis of the information, the principal and classroom teachers all meet to discuss the findings and develop a plan of action. Through several conversations, they collectively realize that many of the teachers have been spending less time during their reading lessons on the meaning and purpose of interpretation. They decide to redesign some of their lessons to focus explicitly on meaning and interpretation exercises.

As the preceding example illustrates, leaders can use CAQDAS software packages to review examples of student work and to calculate coding frequencies from qualitative information. Using ATLAS.ti, or other CAQDAS software, an educational leader can collect, analyze, and interpret student work and other classroom artifacts. Further, the software makes it easy for principals to retrieve portions of student work for inclusion in professional development presentations or in conversations with classroom teachers.

Observing Classroom Instruction and Student Engagement at Westminster High School

ATLAS.ti for the iPad also enables leaders to record audio and video segments using the iPad's built-in camera and then apply codes to the segments of the audio or video file to highlight specific portions of the recordings. This feature was particularly helpful for the instructional coach at Westminster High School. The school enrolls approximately 2,500 students in a ninth-through twelfth-grade configuration.

The district has instructional coaches at the high-school level to help teachers implement the district's new instructional framework. The framework identifies research-based instructional practices that are also linked to the district's teacher evaluation framework. The instructional coach has used ATLAS.ti to visit classrooms and make recordings of teachers who demonstrate effective instruction based on the district's new instructional framework. Her recordings allow her to share best practices and later model effective instructional strategies for all of the school's teachers without requiring them to leave their classroom.

The instructional coach arranged with teachers to visit their classrooms once a day throughout an entire unit. At times, this arrangement meant visiting the teachers' classrooms once, while others required multiple visits. The coach used her iPad video camera to record the teachers teaching for up to 30 minutes when they were engaged in instruction that, based on district teaching rubrics, reflected best practices. The coach then reviewed these recorded segments using ATLAS.ti and coded those sections of the lesson that she felt were illustrative of the type of instruction district leaders desired.

As we noted above, in qualitative analysis, you (as the researcher) can either (a) develop codes as you go along, basing them on what you find in the data, or (b) if you have decided what to look for, create a list of codes ahead of time and then look for examples of them in the data. For our previous example, the principal developed codes as he went along. In this example, the coach began with a coding scheme based on the district's "best-practices" instructional framework.

After reviewing and coding portions of the videos she captured, the coach planned professional development sessions wherein she would highlight portions of the videos to illustrate best practices. During the professional development session, she was able to retrieve coded sections of the video quickly and share these with her colleagues.

Further, given that she had captured multiple teachers engaging in such practices, she was able to highlight how different teachers approached the practices in their classes. In effect, the process simulated the more costly process of having classroom teachers visit each other's classrooms to observe their colleague's instruction.

Teachers who watched the videos asked for additional information, particularly as it related to the impact that these practices have on students. To this end, they asked the instructional coach to record students who were participating in small-group activities to determine which instructional strategies promoted higher levels of engagement in small groups. The coach obliged and thus recorded small-group conversations among students that followed teachers' practices that the coach felt were reflective of best practices from the district's instructional framework.

The coach coded the videos with indicators from the district's instructional framework to highlight which indicators the small-group conversations matched. She then shared the coded segments of the videos with teachers and discussed with them the practices highlighted in the videos and the students' subsequent conversations.

What emerged was surprising. While teachers believed that effective questioning would prompt the greatest levels of student engagement, they found that small-group activities were often preceded with explicit instructions. Teachers were not asking students to explore concepts or discuss issues; rather they were telling them what to do and think. Teachers noted that students, instead of debating various perspectives, tended to seek the "right answer."

As this example illustrates, the ability to retrieve sections of an audio or a video and share them with colleagues creates opportunities to engage in conversations about instructional and leadership practices. This aspect of ATLAS.ti for the iPad may be particularly beneficial for practitioners who are leading professional development. In this example, the use of videos recorded in ATLAS.ti and coded to the district's instructional framework acted like discussion prompts that ultimately led to improved practice. Such dialogue is likely more beneficial when based on actual data rather than on an observer's memory of what transpired.

Improving Principal Support in the District Office at Hillsdale School District

Recognizing the number of initiatives underway in Hillsdale School District, the associate superintendent for Teaching and Learning had become increasingly concerned about the support being provided to the principals. Informal conversations with principals had provided anecdotal information about inconsistent support from key units within the Teaching and Learning Department.

Further, a few principals had expressed concern that the district did not adequately differentiate support for elementary, middle, and high schools. Recognizing these concerns, the associate superintendent decided to send an anonymous survey to all of the district's principals, assistant principals, deans of students, and instructional coaches. The survey used open-ended questions to elicit principals' descriptions of their experiences working with the central office, specifically their experiences with the professional development unit, the assessment department, and the district's five school supervisors.

She received responses from 140 people. After scanning the responses from the survey, she quickly realized that the volume of information she had amassed was unmanageable without some type of software. She used ATLAS.ti for the iPad to read through each of the responses and apply codes to identify the types of support that survey participants felt were needed. She then counted the number of times each code was applied, and she made a display of her counts. She was surprised to find that the type of support requested by participants at the elementary level was significantly different from the type of support secondary campus leaders wanted.

At the district's next school leadership team meeting, which included all of the survey participants plus other administrators in the district, the associate superintendent used the results from her analysis to highlight campus needs the central office staff were not meeting and to initiate a conversation about the ways in they could improve the support to campus leaders.

For example, she noted that principals generally felt that supervisors were largely concerned with implementing the district's new teacher evaluation framework and not as focused on improving the school's test results. Assistant principals perceived that the assessment office was not responsive when they requested data analyses, and so it often fell to them to analyze their own data. Finally, instructional coaches perceived that the central office interacted mostly with principals and assistant principals and rarely recognized coaches' efforts in schools.

Across schools, the associate superintendent perceived differences as well. Elementary principals found the sheer volume of initiatives overwhelming and noted the absence of clear communication from the Teaching and Learning Department. Secondary principals, however, felt they received too little attention and were often left on their own to manage the implementation of new curricula. Drawing from these specific examples, the associate superintendent used the differences she found to begin a series of conversations about the ways in which the department could better serve campuses.

As the example highlights, ATLAS.ti for the iPad provides convenient ways for school and district leaders to learn from qualitative data captured through other technology tools (e.g., the iPad video recorder or SurveyMonkey). Any time text can be exported to a Microsoft Word or Adobe PDF format, ATLAS .ti for the iPad can be used to analyze it.[1] Indeed, the flexibility provided by ATLAS.ti for the iPad to access and analyze qualitative information collected with other tools means that educational leaders have a variety of opportunities to use qualitative information to inform their leadership practice.

CONCLUSIONS

CAQDAS packages such as ATLAS.ti for the iPad provide educational leaders with opportunities to gain insights from the qualitative data in their classrooms, schools, or districts. Such information often richly captures perspectives of key school or district stakeholders and thus can illuminate critical aspects of educational practice. Yet, as we noted at the outset, the absence of convenient tools for educational leaders to use for analysis of such data has meant that managing and interpreting this information was previously very difficult.

We think the opportunities for such analysis using CAQDAS packages are an important development for campus leaders and central office administrators as well. As these vignettes illustrate, ATLAS.ti for the iPad serves as a resource for the collection of data and analysis of the information and as a tool to share selected portions of the data with school staff. Furthermore, in these vignettes we highlight how ATLAS.ti for the iPad prompted educators to begin asking critical questions about their practice. Such questions often lead to instructional improvement, as they are key to improving educators' understanding of their practices.

NOTE

1. ATLAS.ti's desktop version does include a feature wherein you can import survey data in part.

REFERENCES

Anderson, S., Leithwood, K., & Strauss, T. (2010). Leading data use in schools: Organizational conditions and practices at the school and district levels. *Leadership and Policy in Schools, 9*(3), 292–327.

Bauer, S. C., & Brazer, S. D. (2012). *Using research to lead school improvement: Turning evidence into action.* Thousand Oaks, CA: Sage.

Boudett, K. P., City, E. A., & Murnane, R. J. (2014). *Data wise: Revised and expanded edition: A step by step guide to using assessment results to improve teaching and learning* (2nd ed.). Cambridge, MA: Harvard Education Press.

Coburn, C. E., & Turner, E. O. (2011). Research on data use: A framework and analysis. *Measurement, 9,* 173–206.

Denzin, N. K., & Lincoln, Y. S. (2005). *Handbook of qualitative research* (2nd ed.). Thousand Oaks, CA: Sage.

Goldring, E., & Berends, M. (2009). *Leading with data: Pathways to improve your school.* Thousand Oaks, CA: Corwin Press.

Ikemoto, G. S., & Marsh, J. A. (2007). Cutting through the "data-driven" mantra: Different conceptions of data-driven decision making. *Yearbook of the National Society for the Study of Education, 106*(1), 105–131.

Kerr, K. A., Marsh, J. A., Ikemoto, G. S., Darilek, H., & Barney, H. (2006). Strategies to promote data use for instructional improvement: Actions, outcomes, and lessons from three urban districts. *American Journal of Education, 112*(4), 496–520.

Knapp, M. S., Copland, M. A., Swinnerton, J. A., & Monpas-Huber, J. (2006). *Data-informed leadership in education.* Seattle, WA: Center for the Study of Teaching and Policy. Retrieved from http://www.ctpweb.org

Lochmiller, C. R., & Lester, J. N. (2017). *An introduction to educational research: Connecting methods to practice.* Thousand Oaks, CA: Sage.

Luo, M. (2008). Structural equation modeling for high school principals' data-driven decision making: An analysis of information use environments. *Educational Administration Quarterly, 44*(5), 603–634.

Marsh, J. A., Pane, J. F., & Hamilton, L. S. (2006). *Making sense of data-driven decision making in education.* Santa Monica, CA: RAND. Retrieved from http://www.rand.org

Miles, M. B., Huberman, A. M., & Saldaña, J. (2014). *Qualitative data analysis: A methods sourcebook* (3rd ed.). Thousand Oaks, CA: Sage.

Paulus, T., Lester, J. N., & Dempster, P. (2014). *Digital tools for qualitative research.* London, UK: Sage.

Polkinghorne, D. E. (2005). Language and meaning: Data collection in qualitative research. *Journal of Counseling Psychology, 52*(2), 137–145.

Roderick, M. (2012). Drowning in data but thirsty for analysis. *Teachers College Record, 114*(11).

Saldaña, J. (2009). *The coding manual for qualitative researchers.* Thousand Oaks, CA: Sage.

Wayman, J. C., Spring, S. D., Lemke, M. A., & Lehr, M. D. (2012). *Using data to inform practice: Effective principal leadership strategies.* Paper presented at the Annual Meeting of the American Education Research Association, Vancouver, British Columbia.

Wayman, J. C., & Stringfield, S. (2006). Technology-supported involvement of entire faculties in examination of student data for instructional improvement. *American Journal of Education, 112*(4), 549–571.

Young, V. M. (2006). Teachers' use of data: Loose coupling, agenda setting, and team norms. *American Journal of Education, 112*(4), 521–548.

Ysseldyke, J., & Tardew, S. (2007). Use of progress monitoring systems to enable teachers to differentiate mathematics instruction. *Journal of Applied School Psychology, 24*(1), 1–28.

Chapter Three

Classwalk
A Tool to Enhance Instructional Leadership

Sharon Wilbur, Sharon Dean, Leslie Williams, Linda Atkinson, & Jean Cate

KEY POINTS IN THIS CHAPTER

- Research suggests classroom walkthroughs by school leaders can lead to better student achievement.
- Walkthroughs can help administrators and teachers learn more about instruction and identify what training and support teachers need, but many leaders do not use them effectively.
- *Classwalk*, a walkthrough app designed for the iPad, allows one to collect data from classroom visits, summarize the data, and display the summaries.
- *Classwalk* thus facilitates strategic and effective use of the leader's time in doing walkthroughs.
- *Classwalk* is designed around generic research-based instructional strategies, yet is also customizable for specific school needs.

Here, we present information on *Classwalk*, an application for the iPad, to help with classroom observations. We will discuss the research on walkthroughs as a valuable practice, guide you in using *Classwalk*, and suggest how you might find time to use the process and the tool.

A CASE FOR WALKTHROUGHS

Waters, Marzano, and McNulty (2003) identified 21 leadership responsibilities, with each having varying effect sizes for increased student achievement. In later studies, the 21 responsibilities are organized into five dimensions of instructional leadership, three of which have moderate to strong effects on increased student achievement. The three dimensions of leadership are these:

1. Promoting and participating in teacher learning and development;
2. Planning, coordinating, and evaluating teaching and curriculum; and
3. Establishing, communicating and monitoring of goals and expectations (Robinson, Lloyd, & Rowe, 2008).

Educational leaders, charged with multiple responsibilities, would be wise to allocate their precious time to those tasks that yield the greatest rewards in student learning, and these three seem the most promising. Classroom walk-throughs can take just a few minutes and allow principals or other instructional leaders to accomplish tasks in the three dimensions and simultaneously gain valuable data (Cervone & Martinez-Miller, 2007).

Walkthroughs are not the same as observations for teacher evaluation. Walkthroughs promote teacher learning (dimension 1) by monitoring instructional strategies and measuring the level of program implementation on an individual or schoolwide basis. Walkthroughs can also be beneficial when schools have a large number of new teachers and leaders need data for guidance and planning for teacher induction.

In addition, walkthroughs assist in planning, coordinating, and evaluating teaching and curriculum (dimension 2) by providing classroom data as well as schoolwide data. New initiatives at the school, district, or state level can trigger a need for walkthrough data. These initiatives may originate from any event, for example, new grant funding, a literacy initiative, curriculum adoption, or new district/school goals. Each of these initiatives depends upon fidelity of implementation and therefore needs schoolwide monitoring, which can be achieved through the walkthrough process.

Walkthrough data provide a means for monitoring of curriculum and instructional expectations and assist in planning for further teacher learning (dimension 3). Thus, walkthroughs support all three dimensions by gathering data that identify strengths and weaknesses to be used in planning for further teacher learning to improve instruction. But recent research (Grissom, Loeb, & Master, 2013) reveals that walkthroughs alone will not improve instruction. Instead, it is how educators use the data from the walkthroughs that leads to increased learning.

Walkthroughs are meant to help administrators and teachers learn more about instruction and to identify what training and support teachers need (David, 2007). Grissom et al. (2013) assert that unfortunately, the majority of principals use walkthroughs for visibility purposes but do not collect specific concrete data (instead just making "mental notes") and do not use the process to plan for focused professional development.

Some administrators think they are doing walkthroughs when they do formal evaluation observations (Kachur, Stout, & Edwards, 2013). Others do not know what to look for (Pitler & Goodwin, 2008). Many think the process is just too time-consuming and do not understand the benefits. Many do not have a tool customized to their specific needs (Kachur et al., 2013). In this chapter, we introduce such a tool and show how it can help you get the most out of walkthroughs.

CLASSWALK

Because one walkthrough model seldom meets the needs of all leaders, the best tool may be one that involves components shown by research to be effective but that is also easily adaptable to specific local needs (Cervone & Martinez-Miller, 2007). *Classwalk*, a walkthrough app designed for iPad use only, is designed around generic research-based instructional strategies yet is also customizable for specific school needs. Available through the iTunes App Store, *Classwalk* was developed by an educational research organization at a large Midwestern university.

Classwalk is a tool that supports not only the three dimensions of instructional leadership discussed earlier, but also aligns to the International Society for Technology in Education (2007) standards for administrators, McRel's Leadership Evaluation standards (Williams, Cameron, & Davis, 2009), and the Professional Standards for Educational Leaders from the Council of Chief State School Officers (2015). Let us look at how easily the software works.

FOUR FUNCTIONS OF *CLASSWALK*

The front page of the app (figure 3.1) shows four icons that lead to built-in functions for inputting teacher names, developing custom templates, conducting walkthroughs, and creating reports from data analysis.

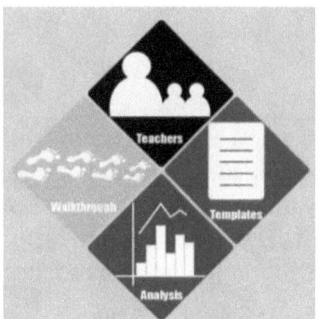

Figure 3.1. Four Functions of *Classwalk*

Function 1: Teachers (Figure 3.2)

The first icon allows for recording of teacher information such as name, grade level, and/or content area.

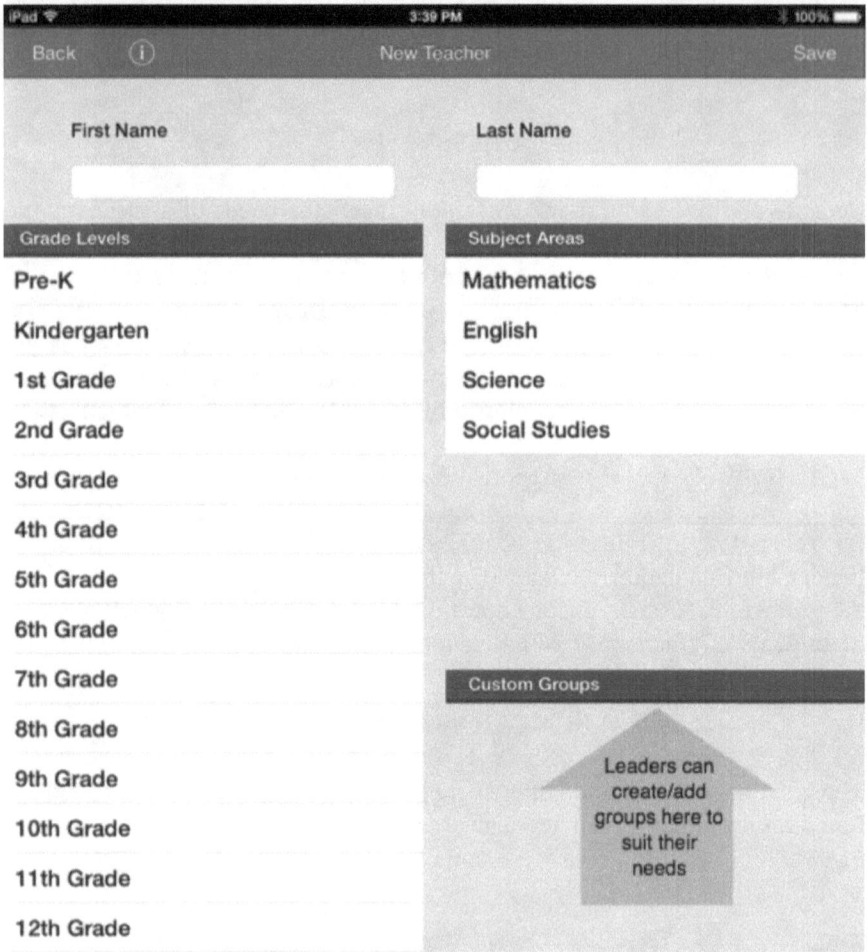

Figure 3.2. Teacher Template

This information becomes useful for later archival and disaggregation of data by teacher or by groups such as grade level or content area. For example, after initiating a literacy program, an administrator may want to see how the program is being implemented at various grade levels. This level of disaggregation requires that teachers be "tagged" by grade level when they are entered into the system.

Later, data can easily be categorized and analyzed according to this information. Analysts can look at groups of teachers categorized by these variables and view evidence of their strengths and their professional growth needs. It is important for leaders to understand, communicate, and model that walkthroughs are not for individual teacher evaluation (Pitler & Goodwin, 2008). However, leaders can use walkthrough data to support individual teacher growth without using the data to evaluate individual performance.

Function 2: Templates (Figure 3.3)

The administrator can organize the observation evidence not only by teacher but also by particular teaching behaviors to be observed. The key to making good decisions based on short three- to five-minute walkthroughs is in the leader's ability to know what to target for observation (Pitler & Goodwin, 2008). Under the "Templates" icon, *Classwalk* contains built-in instructional criteria.

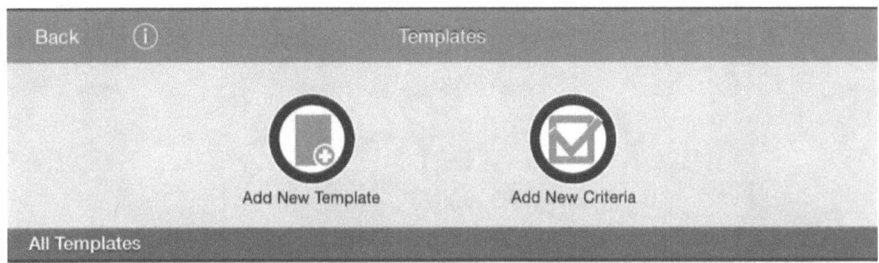

Figure 3.3. Adding New Criteria

An important point is that *Classwalk* is customizable and allows all educators to have a voice in the design of all templates. This voice brings important stakeholders to the table as "doers" rather than those being "done to" (Cervone & Martinez-Miller, 2007; Kachur et al., 2013). Having teacher input into what observers will look for can foster trust in the walkthroughs and credibility for the evidence generated. In addition, one can build, save, and later use templates based on individual school goals or expectations derived from previous professional development.

Then one can use those same templates to monitor the fidelity of teacher implementation of teaching behaviors desired. For example, if a school spent a day of professional development on embedding literacy across all disciplines, a template could be built to monitor the level at which teachers actually are carrying out the practices called for by this approach. If, for example, teachers learned through professional development to embed literacy so students would (a) read analytically, (b) speak on topic, (c) write with evidence, and (d) listen in order to deepen understanding, then each of these could be added as a criterion under a "Literacy" template.

After selecting the "Templates" icon on the home page, the user will have the choice to "Add New Template" or "Add New Criteria." The process of customizing requires that new criteria are added first. One can add criteria by following these steps:

1. Click on "Add New Criteria," which takes the user to the next screen (figure 3.4);
2. Click on "Create New Criteria Type" and (continuing with the example) type "Literacy" in the box. Click "next";

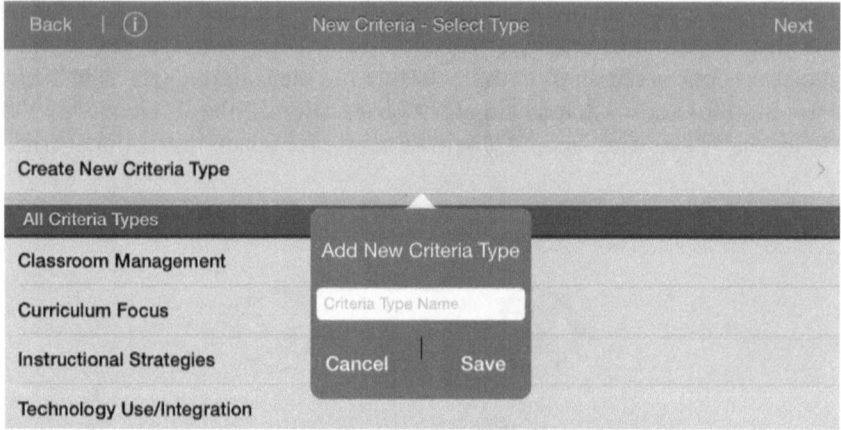

Figure 3.4. Adding New Criteria Type

3. Click on "Criteria Description" (figure 3.5) and type the first criterion for Literacy, in this case, "Reading Analytically";

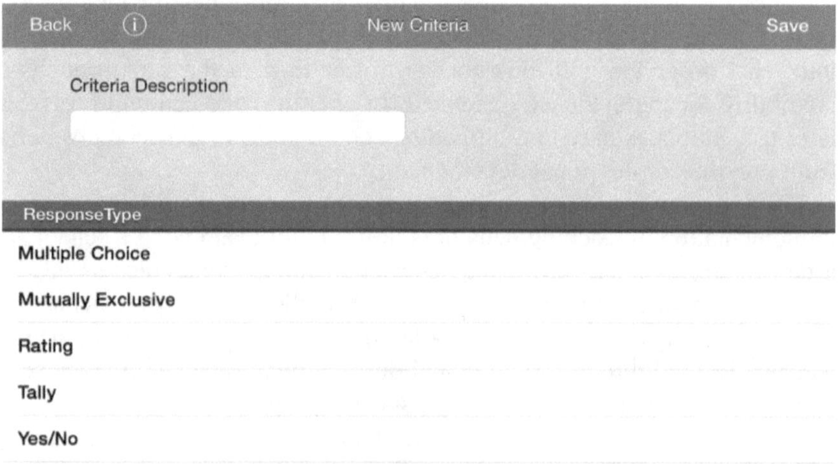

Figure 3.5. Criteria Description

4. Choose the type of data wanted from the list of "Multiple Choice," "Mutually Exclusive," "Rating," "Tally," or "Yes/No."

These choices supply yet another layer of customization for the user. For example, if one just wants to record whether one observes a particular behavior, then the "Yes/No" type would suffice. However, if the user wants to rate the level of analytical reading observed, then the "Rating" type might be better. If a criterion has subsets, they can be added under the "Multiple Choice" type of data. After each of the four components of literacy have been added, each criterion can then be hooked to the "Literacy" template (figure 3.6) and saved for multiple walkthroughs.

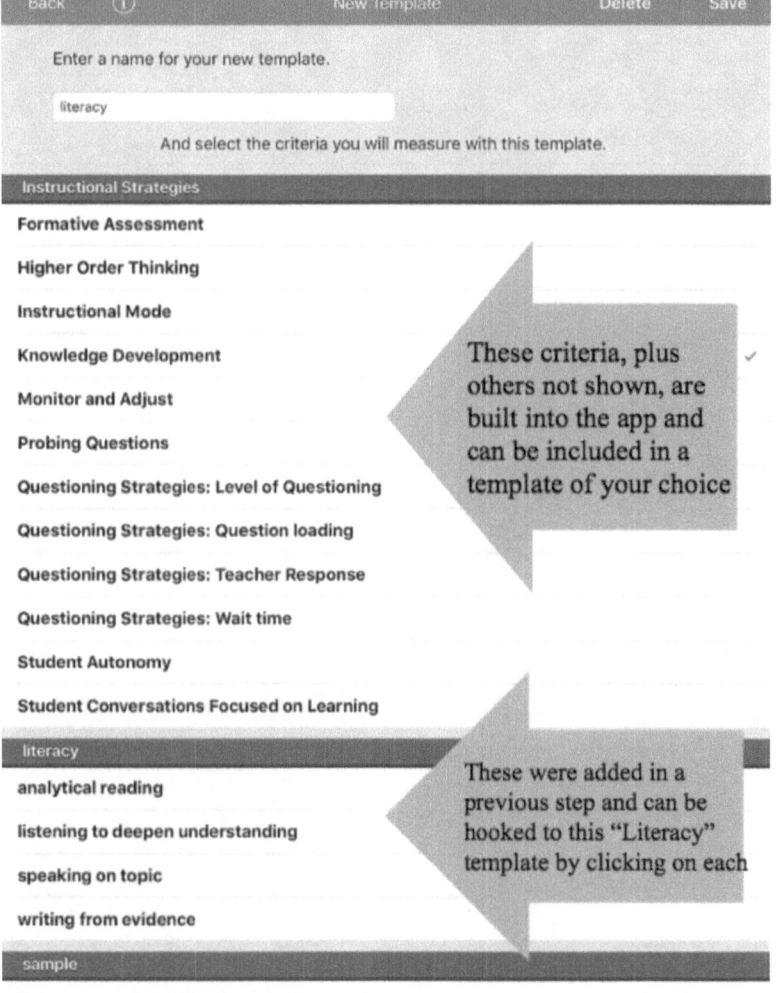

Figure 3.6.   Building Focused Templates

Function 3: Walkthrough

After having downloaded teacher information and templates, the user can access the "Walkthrough" icon to complete as many walkthroughs as desired. The system keeps an archive of each walkthrough completed, the time completed, the teacher involved, and the criteria being observed. One can even take notes by clicking on the "Notes" in the top lefthand corner.

The walkthrough in figure 3.7 is focused on "Tech Use" and is aligned to the International Society for Technology in Education standards for students.

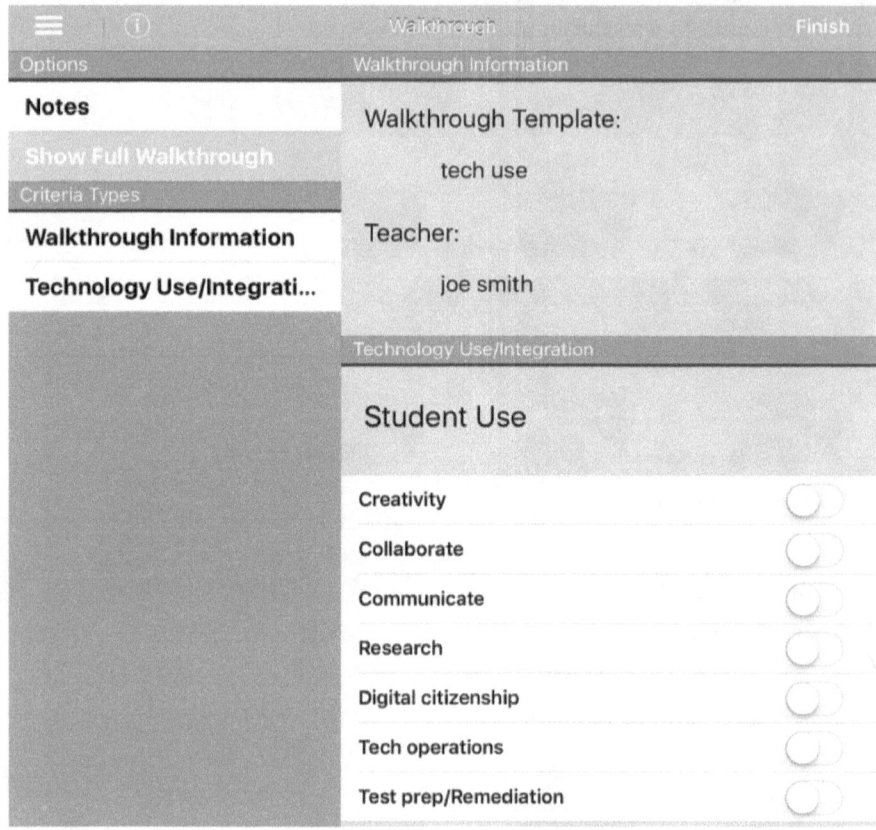

Figure 3.7. Sample Walkthrough Template

Function 4: Analysis (Figures 3.8 and 3.9)

Classwalk generates data charts by template, individual criteria, teacher, or group. As users click each type of chart, they will see choices aligned to that template. For example, if users click on the "Template" choice, they will have the option to disaggregate data by the criteria created. The users can further focus the search by changing the "Start" and "End" dates at the top of the page, yielding data for that template only during the times selected.

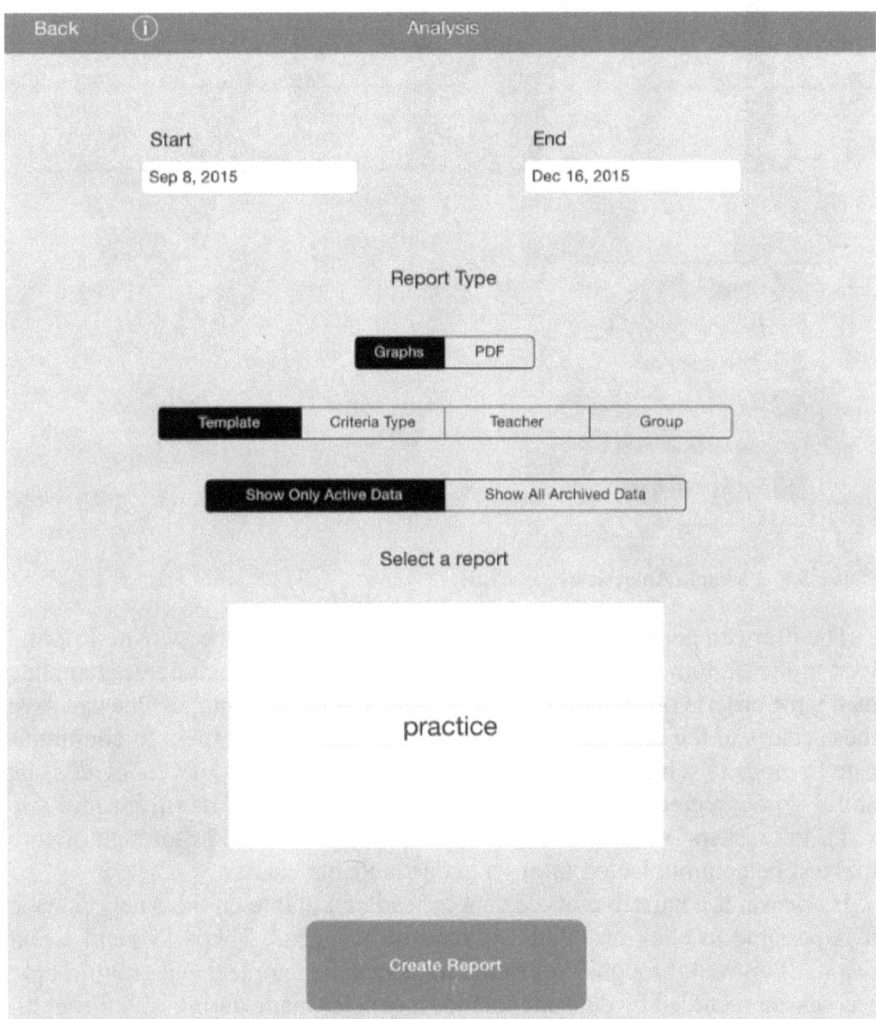

Figure 3.8. Choosing Data Report

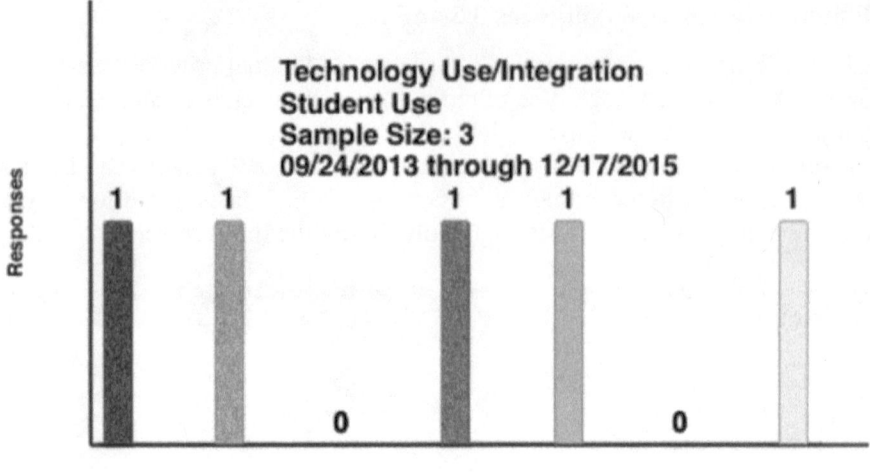

Figure 3.9. Sample Analysis by Template

The user can generate columnar charts by clicking on the "Create Report" icon at the bottom of the page. Charts are in color and include the template name, the criteria observed, the sample size, and the date range. One can save these charts to the photo section of the iPad and/or email them to communicate findings to select people. One of the powerful aspects of *Classwalk* is its ability to aggregate data across teachers and over time. Data from multiple visits to teachers' classrooms provide a more accurate and thorough picture that can be communicated through understandable charts.

If one wants a narrative of the data instead of a graph, on the Analysis page it is possible to click on "PDF" instead of "Graphs." This will yield a text record of all walkthroughs performed for a specific template and group. These records are recorded by date and include any notes made during walkthroughs.

USING WALKTHROUGH DATA

Grissom et al. (2013) found data from a walkthrough model to be effective when it was used to plan focused professional development. *Classwalk*'s developers reported that their own research on *Classwalk*'s contribution to professional development revealed the following:

1. *Classwalk* facilitated the collection of real-time data as opposed to mere impressions;
2. Data from *Classwalk* supported the planning of focused and needed professional development;
3. Walkthroughs with *Classwalk* yielded pre/post evidence of instructional change following the professional development; and
4. *Classwalk* use was perceived as "worth the time."

WORTH THE TIME

In the *Classwalk* developer's study, principals were doubtful at first that they would have time to do walkthroughs in addition to mandated teacher evaluations. But by the end of the study, principals agreed that the time on walkthroughs was well spent, since instruction improved. Grissom et al. (2013) found principals spent the majority of their walkthrough time being "visible." With visibility having only a 0.16 effect size on increased student achievement (Waters et al., 2003), principals would be wise to use the time they are already spending on visibility to collect meaningful walkthrough data.

Many principals have trouble even finding time for visibility. How can principals carve out time from an already busy schedule to do walkthroughs? The following ideas have proven to be successful for others:

- Schedule walkthroughs into a personal calendar on a daily/weekly basis and honor the time scheduled. Many school districts use the McREL leadership evaluation model, which speaks specifically to the need for administrators to persevere in the face of challenges to effectively sustain positive change. Lack of time is a challenge that can be overcome through adherence to an established schedule.
- Share one's calendar with office staff so they can send reminders of scheduled walkthroughs. By communicating to staff the importance of instructional practice, administrators will strengthen a shared belief system necessary for school improvement.

- Make walkthroughs part of annual leadership goals and report monthly progress to the district supervisor. The McREL leadership evaluation model speaks specifically to the importance of monitoring the impact of interventions by collecting data on the performance not only of individuals but also of groups and the school as a whole. The *Classwalk* app facilitates all aspects of this requirement.
- Make walkthroughs collaborative. Invite teachers and other administrators to join in walkthroughs occasionally or to conduct walkthroughs themselves. Walkthroughs can be conducted by trained department chairs and grade level team leaders. Such collaboration will increase a shared understanding of the school, its practices, and its vision for growth.

CAUSAL DATA VERSUS SYMPTOMS DATA

In closing, consider this medical analogy: If a man went to the doctor complaining of constant pain in his left foot, would he not expect the doctor to investigate the cause of the pain? Few doctors would prescribe treatment without looking for an underlying cause. Has the patient acted in such a way to aggravate the foot muscles? Contracted a disease? Had an accident? In other words, what has caused this symptom to appear? The doctor should not try to alleviate a problem without knowing the cause.

Yet administrators may spend much time collecting and analyzing student achievement data without doing a similar examination of the instruction in classrooms. Thus they set out to alleviate a perceived problem of low achievement (for example, having x number of "bubble students") without having identified what caused it. Current scholarship argues that time spent analyzing student achievement data, which are the results (the symptom) of instruction, would be better spent investigating the possible causes of the symptom, including the quality of instruction in the school or grade.

For example, instead of focusing exclusively on remediation, Jensen (2009) asked schools to focus on first-time instruction. Marzano's (2011) causal model supports the notion of leaders focusing their data collection on instruction as a way to reveal possible causes of student achievement. Improved instruction leads to increased student achievement. Effective instructional leadership requires constant attention to "details and undercurrents" (Waters et al., 2003, p. 4) in the classrooms and "uses this information to address potential problems" (p. 4) by "monitoring the effectiveness of school practices" (p. 4).

CONCLUSION

In the foreword to this book, John Nash wrote about how technology can vastly improve human productivity. His example was that humans' ability to move across distances was not very efficient when unaided by technology but that with the invention of the bicycle, that efficiency increased dramatically.

We maintain that administrators doing classroom walkthroughs might be similarly inefficient. But like the bicycle, *Classwalk* can increase human efficiency and usefulness. Performing walkthroughs using an app such as *Classwalk* will provide instructional leaders data on classroom instructional practice that can guide meaningful, focused, and ongoing schoolwide improvement efforts. Rather than just "being visible," school leaders can acquire concrete data on the current state of instruction across classrooms. On the basis of these data, they can provide focused feedback on specific classroom strategies that research suggests can improve student learning. Just like the bicycle, *Classwalk* is a relatively simple, relatively inexpensive technology that can improve our leadership expertise.

REFERENCES

Cervone, L., & Martinez-Miller, P. (2007). Classroom walkthroughs as a catalyst for school improvement. *Leadership Compass*, 4(4).

Council of Chief State School Officers (2015). *ISLLC 2015: Model policy standards for educational leaders*. Retrieved from http://www.wallacefoundation.org/knowledge-center/Documents/Professional-Standards-for-Educational-Leaders-2015.pdf

David, J. (2007). What research says about classroom walk-throughs. *Educational Leadership*, 65(4), 81–82.

Grissom, J., Loeb, S., & Master, B. (2013). Effective instructional time use for school leaders: Longitudinal evidence from observations of principals. *Educational Research*, 42(8), 433–444.

International Society for Technology in Education (2007). *National educational technology standards for administrators*. Retrieved from http://www.iste.org/Content/NavigationMenu/NETS/ForAdministrators/2007Standards/NETS_for_Administrators_2007.htm

Jensen, E. (2009). *Teaching with poverty in mind: What being poor does to kids' brains and what schools can do about it*. Alexandria, VA: ASCD.

Kachur, D., Stout, J., & Edwards, C. (2013). *Engaging teachers in classroom walkthroughs*. Alexandria, VA: ASCD.

Marzano, R. (2011). *The art and science of teaching*. Alexandria, VA: ASCD.

Pitler, H., & Goodwin, B. (2008, Summer). Classroom walkthroughs: Learning to see the trees and the forest. *Changing Schools*, 9–11.

Robinson, V., Lloyd, C., & Rowe, K. (2008). The impact of leadership on student outcomes: An analysis of the differential effects of leadership types. *Educational Administration Quarterly, 44*(5), 635–674.

Waters, T., Marzano, R., & McNulty, B. (2003). *Balanced leadership: What 30 years of research tells us about the effect of leadership on student achievement*. Aurora, CO: Mid-continent Research for Education and Learning.

Williams, J., Cameron, G., & Davis, T. (2009). *McREL's Principal Evaluation System*. Denver, CO: Mid-continent Research for Education and Learning.

Chapter Four

Technology to Enhance Comprehensive Communication

Jon Tienhaara, David Wicks, & Thomas Alsbury

KEY POINTS IN THIS CHAPTER

- Your communications with stakeholders must be flexible, delivered in real time, and customizable.
- Internet technologies allow administrators to present information directly and instantly.
  - Web forms allow data to be collected and accessed digitally for effective use.
  - School leaders need ways of working on documents collaboratively, and cloud technology is a solution to consider.
  - Online spaces may be beneficial for communicating with stakeholders in a timely fashion.
- School administrators need to have an online presence.

School administrators today need to maintain comprehensive and continual communication with multiple stakeholders: teachers, students, parents, community members, and other people interested in the school. Though technology may allow school administrators to enhance communication, they often have little training in the implementation of technology (Flanagan & Jacobsen, 2003).

Coupled with the challenge of providing opportunities for true dialogue with stakeholders is the reality of an increasingly diverse and pluralistic culture. Public demands for accountability and reform initiatives in today's schools require communication efforts to be flexible, delivered in real time, and customized to individual stakeholder groups.

Fortunately, today's technology provides school leaders with opportunities to enhance vertical and horizontal communication, informing stakeholders in real time via whatever device they use to send and receive information. These communication technologies are critical to effective leadership because they allow administrators to collect data, communicate with stakeholders, and facilitate collaboration with internal and external stakeholders from practically any location.

ISTE STANDARDS FOR EDUCATION LEADERS

The International Society for Technology Education (ISTE) has developed standards for education leaders (https://www.iste.org/standards/for-education-leaders). Written to define and encourage the use of technology to improve teaching and learning, these standards describe how school administrators should lead technology-infused school systems. In this chapter, we highlight two ISTE standards for administrators that provide some guidance on how better to lead using specific technology tools.

ISTE Standard 3: Empowering Learning

Standard 3 reads: *Leaders create a culture where teachers and learners are empowered to use technology in innovative ways to enrich teaching and learning.* School administrators should model and promote effective use of technology for learning. They can influence teachers by modeling how technology can improve or benefit teachers' actions.

For example, to increase the overall function of the school, administrators can use technology tools to collect data efficiently in advance of planning and discussions, collaborating with teachers to provide input to school issues in a convenient and secure manner. This collaboration not only helps the administrator create an environment of shared leadership but also models to teachers how specific technologies might also be used for personalized reviews of student progress in the classroom.

ISTE Standard 2: Visionary Planner

Standard 2 reads: *Leaders engage others in establishing a vision, strategic plan and ongoing evaluation cycle for transforming learning with technology.* Schools affect many people, all of whom at one point or another desire information about their schools. As school administrators face these requests, they are expected to provide people with up-to-date and accurate information about vision and strategic planning. Since the Internet enables us to publish information rapidly, school administrators should leverage Internet tools to ensure they provide relevant information to their communities.

School administrators should promote effective communication among school stakeholders using digital-age tools, which we will discuss below, to provide timely, accurate, and useful communication to a broad audience. This allows interested people to receive information in an online space convenient to their specific needs and use. School leaders providing communication through these means, such as blogs, social media, and message boards, are likely to reach an increasing number of stakeholders as people embrace Internet communication tools.

Administrators using these technologies efficiently and effectively can reach many stakeholders (Lovejoy, Waters, & Saxton, 2012). Improved communication with stakeholders can help the school administrator build positive relationships with the community, inform stakeholders of school needs, and bring new school supporters to the table.

In this chapter, in the spirit of the two ISTE standards, we introduce specific technologies that school administrators can use to enhance everyday operations of the school and to work effectively and efficiently. Specifically, we discuss digital data collection, collaborative productivity, and communication.

DATA COLLECTION

School administrators need to collect data from many sources in their organizations and may find real benefits in collecting it digitally. Collecting data digitally makes it easier to collect, store, analyze, and share findings. Following is a typical scenario that illustrates our point.

Case Scenario 1: Preparing for the New School Year

Ms. Green, Skyview Elementary principal, is planning for the upcoming school year. As part of her planning, she will gather feedback from teachers on a variety of issues:

- Teacher "intent to return" for the next school year,
- Teacher reaction to possible change of teaching assignment,
- Teacher input on classroom/curriculum needs, and
- Teacher suggestions on specific student-handbook revisions.

In the past, Ms. Green has collected feedback via discussions at faculty meetings, through talking with teachers during their final evaluation conferences, and in paper forms given to teachers at staff meetings, to be submitted later.

In her view, these methods have been successful. However, she would like to make more efficient use of faculty meetings by collecting teacher input on two issues before the meeting and then using the input to spark discussion. Ms. Green would like to collect teacher data on issues of classroom/curriculum needs and revisions to the student handbook prior to meeting and then summarize the feedback to facilitate collaborative decision making (figure 4.1). In addition to this goal, Ms. Green would like to be able to use these data during district administrative meetings, to illustrate building needs.

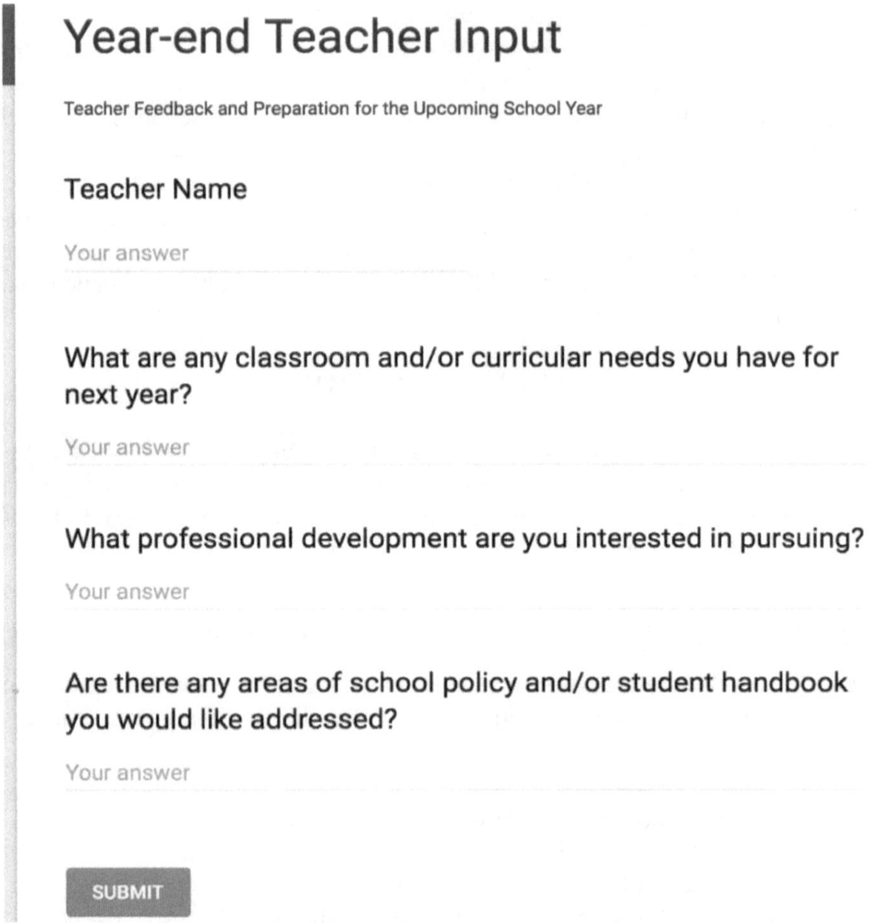

Year-end Teacher Input

Teacher Feedback and Preparation for the Upcoming School Year

Teacher Name

Your answer

What are any classroom and/or curricular needs you have for next year?

Your answer

What professional development are you interested in pursuing?

Your answer

Are there any areas of school policy and/or student handbook you would like addressed?

Your answer

SUBMIT

Figure 4.1. Example of a Web Form Used to Collect Information From Teachers

Application of Technology to Case Scenario 1

Case scenario 1 describes a school principal wanting to engage staff in order to encourage and facilitate staff ownership in readying the school for the next year. This gives teachers the opportunity to contribute ideas and input in an efficient manner, which can lead to more effective schools (DuFour & Mattos, 2013). In case scenario 1, Ms. Green wants to collect various types of information, and she wants to be able to access it digitally for effective use.

Web forms are a technology that is ideal for this purpose. Web forms typically are used to collect simple respondent information, such as opinions, free-form responses, and simple question-and-answer data. Web forms can vary types of questions asked, including multiple choice, text/paragraph box entry, checkbox, list choice, scale, and grid-form questions. Types of questions can be mixed to suit the information needed.

Web forms are customized digital documents that an administrator can send to teachers (and receive back) through email or other Internet means. Examples of web forms include Microsoft Forms (available in Office 365) and Google Forms (available in G Suite). School administrators can use web forms to solicit, collect, store, display, and share a wide variety of data. The school administrator, having determined the type of information to be collected, can then develop the web form (figure 4.2).

After creating the web form, the administrator needs to determine how to send the form to respondents (figure 4.3). Typically, web forms can be published by sending a web address, or Uniform Resource Locator (URL), to people in an email, social network post, or web page. Whichever way you

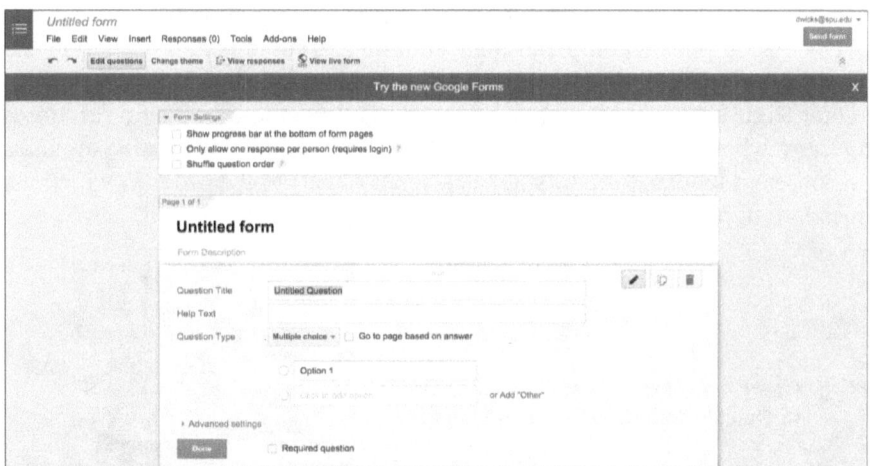

Figure 4.2. An Example of Creating a New Web Form Using Google Forms

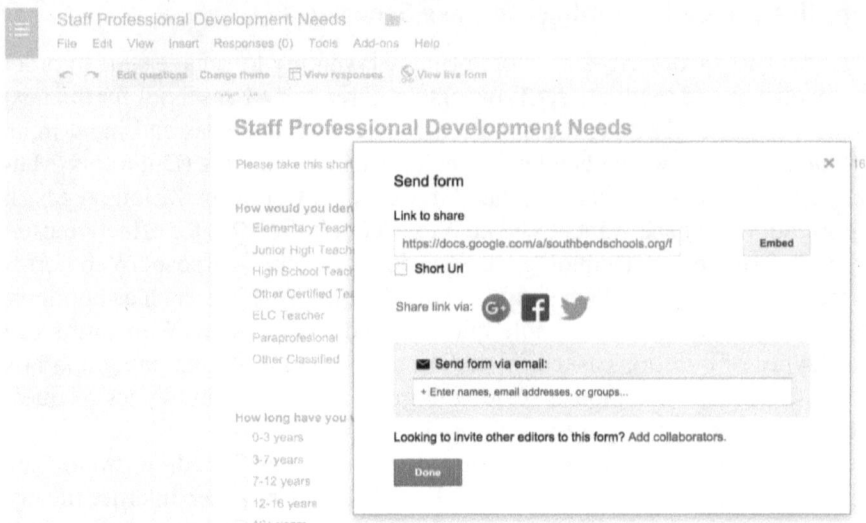

Figure 4.3. Available Options for Sending a Google Form to Survey Participants

use, you send recipients an introductory statement explaining the web form and inviting them to participate. They can follow the link to the web form and answer the questions.

Tip: You can also embed URLs into a Quick Response (QR) code, which can be printed onto a newsletter, flyer, athletic-event program, or bulletin (figure 4.4). Using a smartphone, respondents can scan the QR code and go directly to the web form. This can be useful when soliciting information from the public.

Once a respondent completes the web form and submits it, information and data can be stored in a database or spreadsheet accessible to the web form author (figure 4.5). Most web form programs time-and-date stamp responses to show when they were submitted. Web form programs usually organize responses in tabular format (such as a spreadsheet) in the order in which the questions appeared on the form.

Figure 4.4. Example of a QR Code Used to Quickly Link Documents to Users

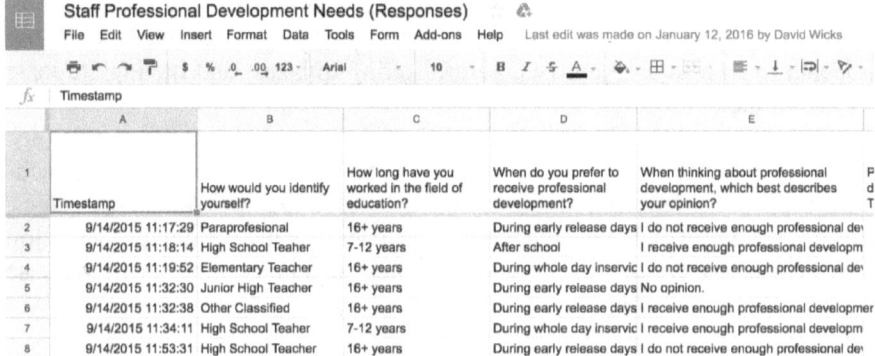

Figure 4.5. Data Collected in a Google Sheet From a Google Form Sent to Survey Participants

The respondents' identifying information can also be collected, though administrators might want to allow people to answer anonymously. Once all respondents have had reasonable time to provide their input, you can go to the spreadsheet or database and analyze the data to present it to intended audiences.

Practical Application of Web Forms for the School Administrator

Here are some specific ways you can use web forms in everyday school situations:

- For staff evaluation purposes, collect preconference and/or postconference information from teachers or staff (lesson plans, learning standards, lesson reflections, etc.);
- Receive input on specific questions or issues prior to a meeting or discussion;
- Survey stakeholders (e.g., parents) about specific topics and then report the results;
- Convert specific paper/carbon forms to "paperless" forms that can be sent/managed digitally (e.g., collecting student information from parents);
- Receive digital files via URL-link submission (e.g., submitting URLs linking to scanned or digital documents);
- Solicit perspectives on professional development (figure 4.5); and
- Record information from classroom observations or notes (also see the chapter on *Classwalk* in this volume, by Wilbur, Dean, Williams, Atkinson, & Cate).

School administrators who learn to use web forms will quickly realize how to adapt them for multiple uses in collecting data. Administrators can then guide teachers on specific classroom applications of web forms. Common examples include collecting student and/or parent feedback, enabling students to turn in assignments, administering quizzes, and having students reflect on their learning.

Administrators should provide training in technology use, security (see Robert F. Hachiya's chapter, this volume), and integration, and provide technical support for learning and using these tools to teachers and staff. Principals can accomplish this by encouraging teacher user groups and participation in professional development courses. In doing so, administrators will increase not only their own efficiency but also that of teachers and staff.

COLLABORATIVE WRITING

School leaders and staff sometimes need to work on documents collaboratively from different locations. Until now, this work might have consisted of the sharing of separate word processing documents (one from each person in the group), resulting in a final integrated product. Rather than people being able to work on one document concurrently, collaboration consisted of independent, tedious work, blind to the contributions of others.

Cloud technology (e.g., G Suite or Office 365) allows for real-time, shared access to a central resource that facilitates collaboration (Kuo, Yu, Yang, Hu, & Yang, 2012) and enables collaborators to share and edit one file seamlessly and in an organized manor. School leaders can use this technology to encourage a team approach that will be efficient and productive.

Collaborators can contribute to working documents from any Internet-able device from any location (figure 4.6). (Editor's note: Figure 4.6 shows a document being worked on simultaneously by two writers. Cursors appear after two lines: one that ends with the words "lockdown drill" and one that ends with the date "May 1–19." In the actual document on screen, these cursors will be two different colors, one for each writer.)

Below are some ways principals and other school leaders can use cloud documents in everyday school situations for collaborative writing:

- Collaborate on the development of meeting agendas;
- Collaborate on documents such as policy manuals, handbooks, and accreditation reports, worldwide if necessary;
- Share documents via URL with stakeholders—through email, social media, QR codes, or websites;
- Create hyperlinked documents with embedded information (meeting agendas, administrative reports, updates, and newsletters); and,
- Access cloud documents and files from any Internet-linked device.

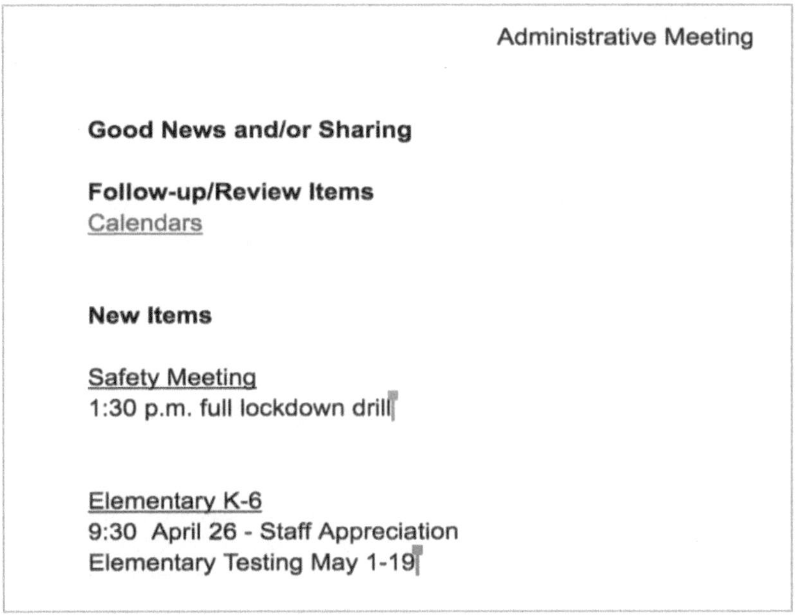

Technology to Enhance Comprehensive Communication

```
                                    Administrative Meeting

    Good News and/or Sharing

    Follow-up/Review Items
    Calendars


    New Items

    Safety Meeting
    1:30 p.m. full lockdown drill


    Elementary K-6
    9:30  April 26 - Staff Appreciation
    Elementary Testing May 1-19
```

Figure 4.6. Colored Cursors Indicating Editors Working on a Cloud Document Simultaneously

Case Scenario 2: Teacher Collaboration

Mr. Lopez, the principal of Highline High School, is forming a Building Improvement Team (BIT) with the goal of increasing staff collaboration and site-based leadership. The BIT will develop curriculum, school budgets, staff resources, the student handbook, and other initiatives. Mr. Lopez hopes staff will experience schoolwide leadership by efficiently contributing to the operation of the school.

Because staff are limited to one half-day in-service per month and bi-weekly meetings after school, Mr. Lopez has little time for staff to collaborate face-to-face on writing. Mr. Lopez would like to find a way for staff to work on project documents without having to meet with one another, where all team members can contribute to and share real-time edits and updates. It is a goal of the BIT for team members to be able to offer suggestions and ideas as working documents are developed and to access the documents off-site at times that are convenient to their busy schedules.

Application of Technology to Case Scenario 2

Case scenario 2 describes a school principal who wants staff to be able to collaborate actively on the development, editing, and sharing of school documents. For teachers and staff to achieve this, it is important for the collaboration to occur in a single document accessible online by those participating in the process, where edits can be seen in real time.

Several online products allow the kind of collaboration seen in case scenario 2. Two of the common ones include G Suite (formerly known as Google Apps) and Office 365, both of which are available to schools at minimum cost. These cloud-based products each include applications for the following: word processing, spreadsheets, presentations, and email. User accounts include access to the applications and a sufficient amount of online storage.

For example, Mr. Lopez and teacher leaders may wish to plan collaboratively for specific meetings. In G Suite, invited users can contribute ideas, questions, or other comments for the rest of the team to review. This allows users to access documents conveniently, and takes advantage of the ubiquitous nature of mobile devices (Dinh, Lee, Niyato, & Wang, 2013).

Multiple writers can collaborate using a cloud-based productivity tool such as G Suite. G Suite uses online documents, spreadsheets, forms, and presentations that can be shared via email. Users can collaborate concurrently, seeing other collaborators' edits in real time. These documents can also be shared via URL, which can be posted to a variety of social media platforms.

This feature allows school stakeholders who use Facebook or Twitter to share documents such as school calendars, bulletins, or any other school forms. The owner of the files can set access restrictions allowing only certain people to view/edit, or authors can open access to the public, accessible by anyone with an Internet connection.

Tip: Using cloud documents allows users to change or update documents after they have been sent out, eliminating the need to publish a new document when changes are made. However, remember to inform viewers that you made a change, either through email or other means.

Cloud documents also provide for easy organization and updating. With a cloud-based document, one online document is shared with collaborators, allowing users to edit one central document. Also, an administrator who may need to change a published document after it has been shared can edit the document accordingly. This way, users accessing the document will see updated changes without having to open or access a separate document, and users will not be confused by varied versions of the developing document.

Another benefit of cloud-based documents is that users can link information into documents using hyperlinks. This option increases efficiency by incorporating into the working document other supporting documents, information, pictures, and media.

For example, Mr. Lopez may share with teacher collaborators in the BIT a draft copy of the next school year's student handbook. This shared document can contain hyperlinks to referenced district policy, state laws, or other related information relevant to the student handbook (figure 4.7). Rather than being limited to the simple mentioning of pertinent information, which requires collaborators to go elsewhere to find the referenced information, cloud documents containing hyperlinked information allow collaborators to view information that is referenced within the cloud document itself.

(Editor's note: Figure 4.7 shows a one-sentence policy on burglary, followed by two underlined references to other documents. On screen, these underlined references will be in color, indicating that they are hyperlinks to sources that back up the policy.) Such hyperlinks can be useful in reducing the need to copy related paper attachments, consolidating related documents into one accessible cloud document, or providing external information or media pertinent to the topic at hand.

		Detention	Suspension (ST)	Suspension (LT)	Expulsion
8	**Burglary:** A student shall not enter or remain unlawfully in a district building with intent to commit a crime. RCW 9A.52.101, RCW 9A.52.060				X
9	**Cheating:** A student shall not knowingly submit the work of others and represent it as his/her own. S/he shall not aid and abet (conspire) the cheating of others. RCW 28A.635.040		X	X	

Figure 4.7. Example of Student Handbook Showing Hyperlinked State Statutes

Practical Application of Cloud Documents for the School Administrator

The ability to share documents with collaborators and simultaneously edit the documents in real time leads to numerous practical applications not possible prior to cloud computing. In addition, the ubiquitous nature of today's technology and numerous interchangeable platforms allow users to access, create, and edit documents conveniently from almost any location.

School administrators using cloud-based documents are discovering their added value to peer collaboration. The ability for an entire staff, or smaller staff teams, to work together on a single document will not only enhance efficiencies during development but may also increase collective creativity and innovation. Collaborators will be able easily to share working documents with others according to specified security access and can update or change document content in real time, which updates all collaborators and viewers simultaneously.

In addition, teachers can use cloud documents to facilitate student work and interact with parents. Schools implementing cloud technology should consider both staff and infrastructure readiness and provide needed resources to ensure efficient adoption (Khajeh-Hosseini, Greenwood, Smith, & Sommerville, 2012).

COMMUNICATION

School leaders face increased demands from stakeholders, including school staff, students, and parents, to provide them appropriate and timely information. As school stakeholders occupy an increasing number of online spaces, they are using these spaces to find and share information (Mangold & Faulds, 2009). It is important for school leaders to publish information in these online spaces, which can include blog posts, social media updates, and other relevant information.

As expectations of increased communication rise, school administrators should take advantage of Internet tools to reach stakeholders quickly and accurately. It is important for school leaders to stay up-to-date as more and more people move to social media for information (Bolton et al., 2013).

Case Scenario 3: Improved Communication

Effective communication is key to any school administrator's success (Davis, Darling-Hammond, LaPointe, & Meyerson, 2005). Superintendent Johnson is implementing a new communications plan in an attempt to increase awareness of school events and other information. The target audience is all district stakeholders, including students, parents, teachers, staff, administrators, and other interested community members.

The superintendent wants to be able to keep stakeholders updated with current information on district issues and hopes to reach a broad range of individuals. The superintendent also wants to receive input from stakeholders and to provide more opportunities for people to express their opinions.

Application of Technology to Case Scenario 3

Means of communication should make it simple to publish relevant information to a wide audience quickly, accurately, and efficiently. We also need to be able to update published information as new developments occur or as circumstances change. Specifically, the administrator can use a delivery approach, a consumer approach, or a hybrid of the two. A hybrid approach may help ensure the widest possible dissemination of information.

In a delivery approach to publishing information, the administrator provides information to specific predetermined contacts. This approach may use email, automated calls, or text messages. For example, the administrator may send information to a specific email list, maybe a group of community stakeholders, or other individuals who regularly want information. Using this approach, the administrator is usually prompted by a specific event or occurrence and sends updated information to a targeted group. The administrator makes a judgment call on who would want the information and strives to deliver the information as needed.

The consumer approach is different. Rather than taking responsibility to deliver information to those who the administrator thinks would want the information, the administrator provides information in a way that can be accessed (or "consumed") by anyone looking for the information. This can be achieved using a variety of tools as described below.

School administrators should consider using aspects of both *delivery* and *consumer* approaches, in a hybrid model. In K–12 school settings, administrators almost always have stakeholder email addresses, phone numbers, and other contact information. However, stakeholders are now expecting also to find information on the Internet through various media outlets. Because of the increasing popularity of mobile devices, information on social media and websites may be easier for them to access.

If administrators want an efficient way to provide information to a wide range of stakeholders, they should publish the information to the areas that stakeholders frequently visit. An increasing number of stakeholders use social media outlets such as Facebook and Twitter as information sources.

If a school administrator uses a cloud document with a connected URL, the cloud documents can be published within Facebook or Twitter, providing a clickable link to the information. Stakeholders can then receive up-to-date information by subscribing directly to the source of information, which could be a Facebook "like" or blog subscription. One benefit of providing information in this manner is that stakeholders themselves will often "like," mark as "favorite," and/or "share" the communication announcement. This effectively spreads the information to a broader audience and may lead to increased interest.

Administrators can also use blogging sites to serve as publishing tools. Common blogging sites include WordPress, Blogger, and Tumblr (figure 4.8). Each of these tools uses a common editing interface with standard word processing features. Another useful feature of using a blogging tool is that the

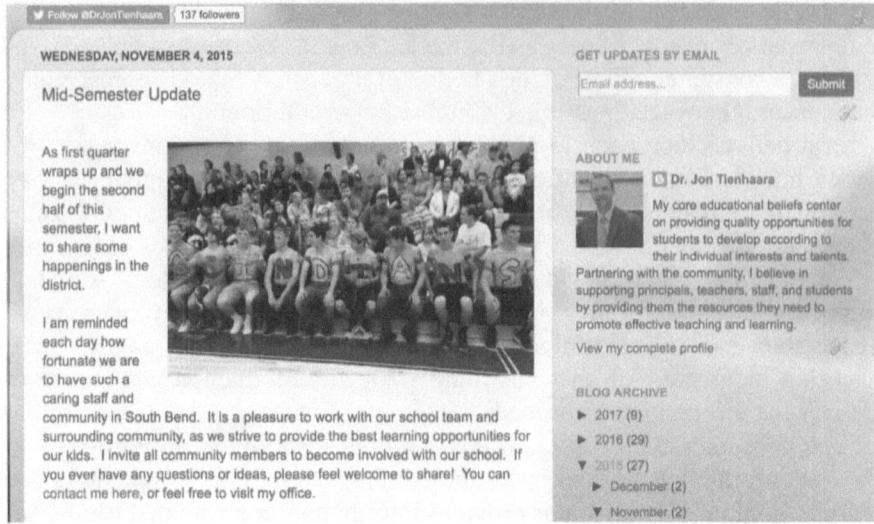

Figure 4.8. Example of How Dr. Jon Tienhaara Uses a Blog (Blogger) to Communicate with Stakeholders

completed blog document can be published to all social networking sites simultaneously, creating a central location for information. Administrators can publish information using one communication tool that effectively reaches stakeholders on all popular social media and web networks.

Tip: Once your online presence is established, be sure to publish regular communication in a consistent manner. Regular publishing will build a "following" of stakeholders who will further share your key information. Calendaring tools can help remind you to post updated content.

Practical Application of Internet Communication for the School Administrator

School administrators need to have an Internet presence. Whether through a school and/or district website, social media account, or blog, the administrator needs to have information available to stakeholders active in these Internet spaces. This presence increases the perceived transparency of the school administration and allows for increased interaction between the administrator and stakeholders.

Below are some specific ways principals, program directors, and district office staff in everyday school situations can use the Internet to communicate with stakeholders:

- Create an official school Facebook account and/or Twitter account, and use these accounts to provide daily updates, pictures of school events, and information;
- Publish a weekly blog of school updates and events; then link the blog to Facebook, Twitter, and the school website;
- Publish the school's daily bulletin or announcements using a blogging site; then link the blog to Facebook, Twitter, and the school website; and
- Use a blog to communicate school updates and information with teachers, students, and staff.

As communication technology changes and advances, school leaders should adapt their communication methods to meet the needs and expectations of all stakeholders. As people move to social networking sites and blogs to communicate and to search for information, school leaders should consider whether or not they have an adequate presence in such sites and blogs. The ease of integrating multiple communication tools allows for an efficient manner of providing information to various online venues.

MATTERS OF PRIVACY

Each of the tools mentioned above uses technology in ways to enhance productivity. However, using Internet applications introduces various risks that you must consider. For example, cloud documents work well to encourage collaboration but must be secure in order to prevent use by unauthorized persons or in unauthorized ways. Internet-based documents can be easily shared and transmitted to a wide audience both intentionally and unintentionally.

Administrators should be careful to ensure online accounts are secured with appropriate and adequate passwords and that they follow district policy concerning privacy matters related to online content. See Robert F. Hachiya's chapter in this volume for more information.

CONCLUSION

As technologies continue to evolve, so do their implications for education. School administrators should remain current on technologies that have the potential to increase the effectiveness of not solely their back-office functions but also the effectiveness of teaching and learning.

REFERENCES

Bolton, R. N., Parasuraman, A., Hoefnagels, A., Migchels, N., Kabadayi, S., Gruber, T., ... & Solnet, D. (2013). Understanding Generation Y and their use of social media: A review and research agenda. *Journal of Service Management, 24*(3), 245–267.

Davis, S., Darling-Hammond, L., LaPointe, M., & Meyerson, D. (2005). *Developing successful principals*. Stanford Educational Leadership Institute. Retrieved from https://edpolicy.stanford.edu/publications/products/949

Dinh, H. T., Lee, C., Niyato, D., & Wang, P. (2013). A survey of mobile cloud computing: Architecture, applications, and approaches. *Wireless Communications and Mobile Computing, 13*(18), 1587–1611.

DuFour, R., & Mattos, M. (2013). How do principals really improve schools? *Educational Leadership, 70*(7), 34–40.

Flanagan, L., & Jacobsen, M. (2003). Technology leadership for the twenty-first century principal. *Journal of Educational Administration, 41*(2), 124–142.

Khajeh-Hosseini, A., Greenwood, D., Smith, J. W., & Sommerville, I. (2012). The cloud adoption toolkit: Supporting cloud adoption decisions in the enterprise. *Software: Practice and Experience, 42*(4), 447–465.

Kuo, L. H., Yu, J. C., Yang, H. H., Hu, W. C., & Yang, H. J. (2012). A study of creating technology education course for cloud computing. *International Journal of Communications, 6*, 98–108.

Lovejoy, K., Waters, R. D., & Saxton, G. D. (2012). Engaging stakeholders through Twitter: How nonprofit organizations are getting more out of 140 characters or less. *Public Relations Review, 38*(2), 313–318.

Mangold, W. G., & Faulds, D. J. (2009). Social media: The new hybrid element of the promotion mix. *Business Horizons, 52*(4), 357–365.

Chapter Five

Searching, Curating, and Networking

Set Up the Tools and Develop the Skills to Make the Modern Web Work for You

Julia L. Parra

KEY POINTS IN THIS CHAPTER

- First, set up your toolkit with four online tools:
  - Google provides a rich set of tools to help us navigate, use, communicate, and create.
  - Twitter is one of the top-ranked social networks on the Internet.
  - As the largest social network, Facebook provides a venue for members to engage in both personal *and professional* interactions.
  - Pinterest is an incredibly popular website and is often referred to as a virtual bulletin board.
- Three key skills are searching, curating, and networking:
  - Searching enables us to find information quickly. It is worthwhile to develop sophistication with searches.
  - Curating enables us to keep track of and organize the resources we find in our searches.
  - Networking involves developing our personal learning environments (PLEs) and our personal learning networks (PLNs).

With access to a world of information via the Internet and powerful tools, you, today's administrators and school leaders, have incredible resources and opportunities at your fingertips. With just your smartphone and a few key skills, you have a world of information available at a moment's notice. Unless it is triple top-secret, you can learn just about anything. If information and knowledge are power, then at no time in history has the average person had access to so much power—or at least the *potential* for power.

To harness this power potential of the Internet, you need tools and you need skills. The tools are there: Multitudes have been created and are being created. These tools are categorized in many ways: Web 2.0, social networks, social media, multimedia, personal learning environments (PLEs), personal learning networks (PLNs), learning management systems, and more. Some of the most popular web apps right now include Twitter, YouTube, Google Search, Google Docs/Drive, Facebook, Pinterest, Instagram, Diigo, and Skype (Hart, 2014a).

But forget the lists; what it comes down to is this: These tools are all part of the "modern web." They are incredibly powerful, and it is time you made them work for you! Okay. Many of you are overwhelmed right now by such lists of tools, lists of tasks, and lists of skills. They may look like they will give you more work to do when you can barely cope with the work you have now. But stick with it; in this chapter you will learn, step-by-step, the key tools and skills you need to make the modern web work for you.

This chapter is in two parts. In part 1, you will *set up your toolkit* with four powerful online tools: Google/Google Search, Twitter, Facebook, and Pinterest. If you are already using these tools, then you can move on to part 2, where you will use your toolkit to *develop three key skills*: *searching, curating, and networking*. A few tips to consider as you embark on this adventure:

1. Keep a physical or digital journal with reflections and important notes.
2. Do an overview of this entire chapter. Use your journal to take notes and reflect.
3. Establish your goals and a plan for developing your skills. What tool do you need the most or which appeals to you the most? Start with that.
4. Focus on one tool at a time.
5. Spend 15 to 30 minutes a day, three to five days a week, developing your skills.

PART 1: SET UP YOUR TOOLKIT

You will start by developing your basic toolkit to include Google, Twitter, Facebook, and Pinterest. Two points: First, note that these four tools are under continuous development and the features discussed here could be different tomorrow; second, always keep in mind that your online identity is very valuable. Protect your personal information, be selective and purposeful with your posts and contributions, establish boundaries, and do only what you are comfortable doing.

Start with these tools on your desktop or laptop computer and then add them to your mobile device(s). Additionally, you need to establish how you will remember the usernames and passwords that you create for your new tool accounts.

Get Started with Google/Google Search

The Internet is everything! And Google provides a rich set of tools to help you navigate, use, communicate, and create web pages. Google Search is the Internet search engine that has become a daily tool and even has its own verb: "Just Google it." With Google Search, you have the power of the Internet and access to the world of information at your fingertips if you carry a smartphone/phablet or keep close at hand a computing device (tablets, laptops, desktops).

Google Search provides immediate means to research any topic using descriptive words, phrases, sentences, and questions. If your device has a microphone, you can even search by voice rather than by typing in terms. Google Search integrates with your Google account and provides personalization features, especially if you use the Google Chrome browser. Whether you need resources now or later, the best place to start finding them is on the Internet with the number one search tool: Google Search. To get started:

1. Note that you do not need to create an account with Google to use Google Search. Just go to http://google.com and locate the search box in the middle of the page. Once you conduct a search, the search box is at the top of the page. Try searching for Google Search tutorials, and pick a couple to read or watch.
2. If you have a Gmail account that you use for email, you already have a Google account. When you are signed into your Gmail or Google account, you have access to many resources. When you are logged into your Gmail/Google account, look to the upper right corner, there is a small three by three grid (some people call it "the waffle"); click on that to access basic Google tools, including Search.
3. If you don't have a Google account and want one, go to https://myaccount.google.com and select "Create Your Google Account." You can have multiple Google accounts. For example, if you want a Google account just for testing tools, you can create one. If you will also use this Google account for professional purposes, consider using your real name as your username or as close to it as you can.

4. When you sign up for online tools, you are usually asked to provide an email address. Consider using your Google email (which is referred to as "Gmail") as your email address for the rest of the tools you add to your toolkit.
5. Now that you can use Google Search, it is helpful to note that if a question comes up or if you need something demonstrated, you can always Google it! For example, the next tool you will learn about is Twitter. Type into Google Search, "Twitter tutorial," and right away, relevant and helpful video tutorials will come up.

Get Started with Twitter

Posts made on Twitter are limited to 280 characters; thus, Twitter is a microblogging tool, and since it is used for global interaction and communication, it is also a social network. Twitter is one of the top-ranked social networks on the Internet and was voted by educators around the world the number one tool in the Top 100 Tools for Learning 2014 published by the Centre for Learning and Performance Technologies (Hart, 2014a). Twitter is often viewed as frivolous and a recreational tool for teenagers, but dig a little deeper and you will see that Twitter is an incredibly powerful and empowering tool for a variety of audiences, including educators. To get started:

1. Join Twitter at http://twitter.com. Note that you have both an @username that becomes part of your URL and you have an account name that is part of your profile information (i.e., mine are @desertjul and https://twitter.com/desertjul). Most professionals use their real name for the account name for optimal professional networking.
2. You will be asked for an email account. Consider using your Gmail as your email address for this.
3. You will be prompted to follow some prominent and interesting Twitter users; you should follow some that appeal to you. You can always unfollow later if you want. Following are a few recommendations. Click the Follow button on their pages:
    a. U.S. Department of Education, https://twitter.com/usedgov;
    b. An administrator, George Couros, https://twitter.com/gcouros;
    c. A high-school principal, John Robinson, https://twitter.com/21st principal;
    d. A creator of #edchat and education author, Shelly S. Terrell, https://twitter.com/shellterrell;
    e. Edutopia, which has many great resources, https://twitter.com/edutopia;

- f. See 50 Educator Twitter Accounts Worth Following, http://www.teachthought.com/uncategorized/50-educator-twitter-accounts-worth-following/;
- g. As you engage with districts, schools, and school leaders you admire, look them up to see if they are on Twitter;
- h. If a link in this section doesn't work, remember, you can Google it! or search for anything directly in Twitter with the search bar in the upper right of the Twitter page.

4. If you haven't added pictures, click on your own name to go to your profile page and click Edit Profile and update with your pictures and anything else you missed.
5. Take some time to explore further the tools on your Twitter page: Home, Moments, Notifications, and Messages.
6. Click on your small picture in the upper right and explore the tools that drop down. These are your Settings and deserve some time. Make sure all of your settings are where you want them. In the Privacy setting, if you select "Protect my Tweets," it is complicated to participate in networking activities; consider being public, not private.
7. Practice searching in Twitter now. As you start using the Twitter Search tool in the upper right corner, you will start to understand the power of Twitter for networking. Of note, Twitter might allow only 280 characters, but people can do a lot with that, including linking to more substantive resources like blogs, videos, podcasts, articles, and so on.
   - a. Search for and explore some hashtag conversations for administrators. Hashtags allow you to join existing conversations about a topic. Some of the top hashtags for administrators (Bhaskar K, 2013) include #cpchat, which stands for Connected Principals, #edleaders, #edadmin, #edpolicy, #edreform, #k12, and #edchat. As you explore these hashtag conversations, you will find more Twitter accounts to follow and possibly more current and relevant hashtags.
   - b. You can also search for topics of your own choosing as well as create a hashtag topic of your own. For example, #NMSULDT is a program hashtag being used to post resources for students.
8. As you find "tweets" that you find useful or meaningful, consider using the tools under the tweet to
   - a. Reply with your own thoughts in 280 characters or less;
   - b. Retweet to share the tweet on your Twitter profile page; or

c. "Like," which validates the person you are "liking." The "like" feature is a heart. When you go to your profile page, the tweets you "like" will be in your Likes feature.
9. The number of Twitter accounts that you will follow may grow rapidly. At this point, you can create some lists to keep organized and view focused sets of tweets. Click on your own name to go to your Home page, select Lists and then "Create a list." You could also create a list of your own teachers and staff.
10. Finally, take that brave step if you have not already, and compose a new 280-character tweet. You can use the box that's titled "What's happening?" You can also click the tweet box in the far upper right.

Get Started with Facebook

As the largest social network, with over a billion and a half members, Facebook provides a venue for members to engage in both personal and professional interactions. Facebook provides multiple ways for doing so, including adding friends, creating and liking pages, creating and joining interest groups, interacting with game apps, participating in events, and communicating via the Messenger tool. To get started:

1. Sign up with Facebook at http://facebook.com. Most professionals use their real name for optimal professional networking.
2. You will be asked for an email account. Consider using your Gmail as your email address for this.
3. Facebook will guide you in finding your friends and filling out your profile. Do what feels comfortable to you, and skip anything you don't want to do. You can always edit later with the Edit Profile feature in the upper left on the Home page.
4. On your Home page you will see all of the posts of your friends and the pages you follow.
5. Here are a few recommendations of Facebook pages to follow:
   a. Facebook for Educators, https://www.facebook.com/FBforEducators/;
   b. Edutopia, https://www.facebook.com/edutopia/;
   c. As you engage with districts, schools, and school leaders you admire, look them up to see if there are pages to follow or leaders to add as friends.
6. In the upper left and upper right corners, you can click on your name to see your page and posts. Here you can also click the three dots next to View Activity Log and access Timeline Settings. (These are also acces-

sible from the little dropdown arrow in the upper right.) Spend some time here. Revisit often.
7. In the beginning, be very selective about who you add as "Friends." You don't have to friend your teachers, staff, students, and parents. However, over time, if you decide this is something you might want to do, use your Google Search skills to learn more about the best ways to add teachers, staff, students, and parents. Also, Facebook has a search bar at the top to find people and resources on Facebook.
8. You can create your own posts by using the box at the top that says, "What's on your mind?"

Get Started with Pinterest

Pinterest is an incredibly popular website and is often referred to as a virtual bulletin board. Pinterest provides a visual discovery experience, allowing users to collect, share, and store visual bookmarks that link to web resources; this is done by "pinning" visual bookmarks to "boards" of interest. Pinterest promotes the use of visually appealing images. Some of these images link to further information. And some of these images are in the format of infographics; infographics (or "information graphics") can provide complex information in a meaningful, easily consumed way. To get started:

1. Sign up for an account at https://pinterest.com. You do have the option to sign up using either your Facebook or Twitter account. For personal cybersecurity purposes, you should create a unique account for each tool you use. You can connect your social accounts later.
2. Most professional users provide their real names. And again, you will be asked for an email account and should consider using your Gmail as your email address for this. Also consider using the same username you used with Twitter. Like Twitter, you have a username and account name.
3. When you are exploring in Pinterest, note that you can follow Boards or people.
4. One helpful feature to use is the Pinterest browser button. On your own profile page, find "Visit the Help Center." Select "Pinterest basics" and "All about the Pinterest browser button." The Help Center is a great resource!
5. For many more tips, review Edutopia's resource titled "20 Top Pinterest Tips" (Davis, 2015).

Remember that all of these tools evolve quickly. When this chapter is published, the features for any of these tools are likely to be different. If that's the case, then (a) Google it! and (b) know that all of these tools have "Help" features.

PART 2: DEVELOP THREE KEY SKILLS—SEARCHING, CURATING, AND NETWORKING

As a school leader, you take on many roles and tasks to support all of the stakeholders in your school(s). George Couros (2012) notes that as a division principal, two of the most important administrative tasks or roles he fulfills are (a) building relationships and (b) serving as an instructional leader. These types of administrative tasks/roles will be the focus in this chapter as relevant and common administrative scenarios are used to help you develop three key skills.

Three key skills are (a) searching for information and resources, (b) curating the information and resources you find, and (c) networking for professional growth. You will engage with the four tools you previously added to your toolkit—Google Search, Twitter, Facebook, and Pinterest. When screenshots are provided, it is important to note that they are relevant to give you a feel for the tool but that these types of tools change constantly and the screenshots quickly become outdated.

Skill 1: Searching for Information and Resources

Patterson (1993) says instructional leaders are resourceful, and Whitaker (1997) identifies two resource-focused skills of instructional leadership: being a resource provider and being an instructional resource. In the latest version of standards from the Interstate School Leaders Licensure Consortium, almost every standard upholds the importance of promoting "*each* student's academic success and well-being" (National Policy Board for Educational Administration, 2015, emphasis original).

Willison (2008) said that an effective instructional leader needs to "talk the talk," as an "expert on teaching and learning" with an "informed vocabulary of pedagogical terms." Willison adds that such a leader must also "be the caddy," that is, carry the bag and provide advice on the shots and club selection. In other words, as an instructional leader, you need information and resources at your fingertips for yourself and for your learning communities.

In the following scenario, you will learn to search for information and resources with three of the tools in your toolkit—Google Search, Twitter, and Facebook. Read Kevin Badgett's chapter in this volume for further insights and information.

Administrative Scenario: Searching for Resources for Your Upcoming Professional Development Meeting

Imagine it is early in the spring semester and in three weeks, you, as instructional leader, are scheduled to join a team of teachers participating in an upcoming pilot to deploy one-to-one Chromebook use in classrooms during the fall semester. The teachers are engaging in professional development about using collaborative tools and increasing collaborative teamwork in their classrooms with the Chromebooks.

At this first meeting, you will all share resources and start planning for the one-to-one Chromebook deployment with a focus on collaboration. Remember that you need resources for yourself to "talk the talk" and you need current resources to share with your teacher team. It is time to start searching. First, Google it!

Google It

If you are on a laptop or desktop using Google Chrome, you can type right into the URL bar or in the Google Search bar that comes up with every new window. Notice your microphone tool on the right, in case you want or need to use the voice feature. If you are not using the Google Chrome browser, type google.com in the URL bar. Try a text-based search, and type into the URL bar the following: "best collaboration tools and strategies for chromebooks in K12." Quotes are used here to demonstrate search strings and terms, but the quotation marks are not necessary.

On a smartphone, the voice feature can be used to speak the same phrase. As a busy administrator, you might be fully mobile and can use your smartphone/phablet or other computing device. You just need a browser tool. With Google, you can use brief terms, short sentences, questions, and basically anything that works for you.

Note that you might achieve different results on desktop vs. iPhone, but on the first page of each search there should be at least two resources that will help with (a) increasing professional vocabulary for conversation and (b) having some resources to share with the team of teachers. Note that at the top of your Google Search results, there are filters: All, Shopping, News, Videos, Images, More, and to the right: Settings and Tools. If you click on Tools, two additional filters, "Any time" and "All results" come up (see figure 5.1). Over time, get to know these filters and options.

You can dig deeper by:

1. Clicking through more pages at the bottom of the page,
2. Using the list of related clickable searches near the bottom, and/or
3. Trying a different search term, phrase, or question.

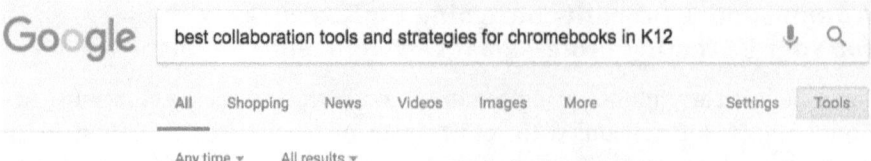

Figure 5.1. Google Search and Filters Screenshot

Remember to set aside and schedule time to practice your Google Search skills. Just 15 to 30 minutes, three to five days a week is an excellent goal. Soon you will find yourself telling others, "Just Google it!"

With this scenario complete, you can now talk the talk and you have a few great resources to share. Google Search is an excellent starting point, but don't forget your recent explorations with Twitter and Facebook and how they can connect you to the people who are contributing to a topic right now. Over the next few days, you will continue your searching by using Twitter and Facebook.

Twitter Search

For Twitter searches, you want to use shorter terms as keywords such as "chromebooks collaboration," "K12 collaboration," "collaboration tools," "Google collaboration tools," "chromebooks," and "collaboration." Again, the quotes demonstrate search strings and terms, but you will not use them to search. Note that at the top of the Twitter search results, you have options to filter your results: Top, Latest, People, Photos, Videos, News, and Broadcasts. Over time, get to know these filters (see figure 5.2).

When searching for "chromebooks collaboration" using Twitter Search, some hashtags in the results will include #chromebooks and #collaboration. When a concept is hashtagged, it is clickable and can lead to further resources and exploration. Scrolling through the tweets on these topics will result in related images that serve as excellent resources, demonstrating the physical environments involved with Chromebooks and collaboration.

To gather (curate) and share tweets of value, consider retweeting and liking your favorites and adding your own hashtag so that when you search

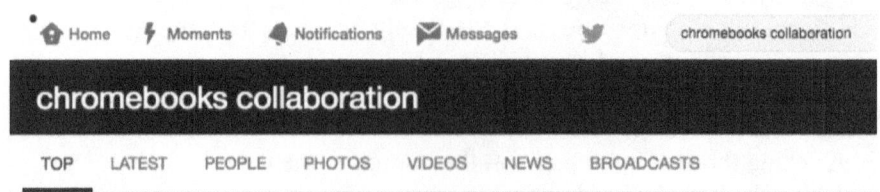

Figure 5.2. Twitter Search and Filters Screenshot

your hashtag you can find your favorite tweets again. Also, if your teachers use Twitter, they can contribute resources with the same hashtag. And vice versa, ask your teachers if they are using particular hashtags that you can use to support their work.

Facebook Search

For Facebook searches (facebook.com) as with Twitter, you want to use shorter terms as keywords such as "chromebooks collaboration," "K12 collaboration," "collaboration tools," "Google collaboration tools," "chromebooks," and "collaboration." Again, quotes are used here to demonstrate search strings and terms but are not necessary for a search. Note that at the top of the Facebook search results, you have options to filter your results: Top, Posts, People, Photos, Videos, Pages, Places, Groups, Apps, and Events. Over time, explore all of these filters (see figure 5.3).

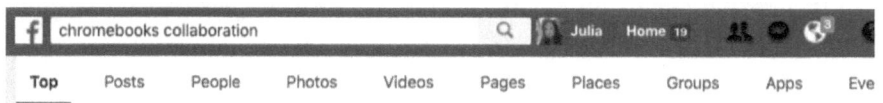

Figure 5.3. Facebook Search and Filters

To gather (curate) the resources that bring you value, there is a tiny drop-down arrow in the upper right of a resource, with the option to "Save post," "Save link," and the like (see figure 5.4). When you are back at your Home page, on the left, select "Saved" to view your saved resources.

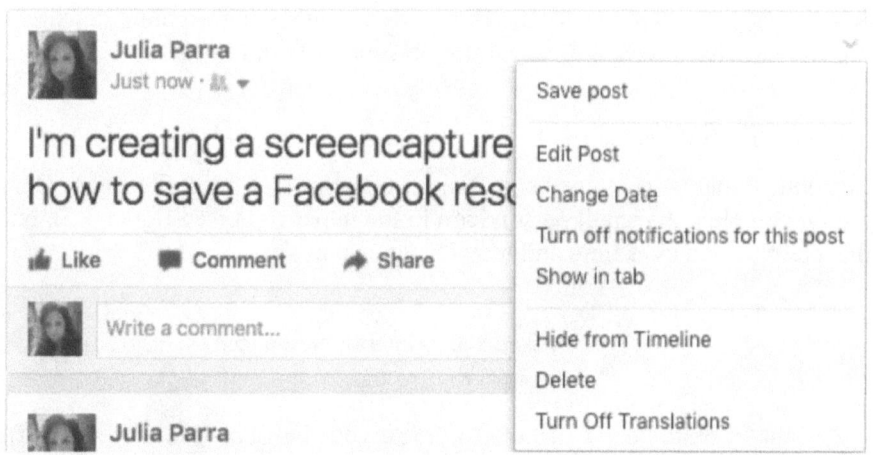

Figure 5.4. Save Facebook Resources

Skill 2: Curating the Great Resources You Are Finding

You have started using new tools and you have developed your searching skills. You might be overwhelmed by the amount of information and resources you have realized are available to you. At this point it would be helpful to develop some curation (gathering and tracking) skills. Curation skills are vital to avoid "data overload" and "digital hoarding" (Heick, 2013, section 4) as well as promoting peace of mind in the knowledge that you can find a resource or set of resources when you need it. Of course, you could just "Google it" again, but there are more efficient ways.

The skills related to curation include "collection, display, and labeling of information" (EDUCAUSE, 2012, p. 1), and the current tools commonly used to curate from the modern web include "Pinterest, Scoop.it, Learnist, Tumblr, Storify, and Educlipper" with their "pin-board" type interfaces (EDUCAUSE, 2012, p. 1). The previous scenario continues wherein you will start developing your curation skills with one of the tools in your toolkit: Pinterest. You will use Pinterest to search for resources and curate those resources by creating your first Pinterest board.

Administrative Scenario: Curating the Resources for Your Upcoming PD Meeting

In two weeks, you are scheduled to join your team of teachers participating in an upcoming pilot to deploy one-to-one Chromebooks for use in their classrooms during the fall semester. Remember that they are engaging in professional development about using collaborative tools and increasing collaborative work in their classrooms with the Chromebooks. You are still developing your searching skills. This week you are going to continue searching and practice a new skill of curating resources with Pinterest.

Curate with Pinterest

Log into Pinterest (pinterest.com) and navigate to your profile page. Currently, you click the small person icon in the upper right (see figure 5.5), but this has changed over time and may change again.

Figure 5.5. Pinterest Person Icon

Use the "Create board" feature to create your first board (see figure 5.6). When naming your board, consider a name that would allow you to share your board with various audiences, such as, "Chromebook Collaboration Tools." Select "Create."

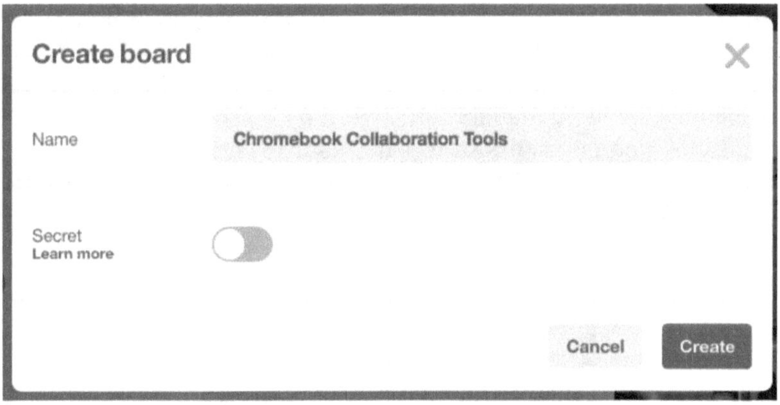

Searching, Curating, and Networking 67

Figure 5.6. Create Pinterest Board

Once your board is created, you can always hover your mouse over the board and select "Edit" to add a description, category, or other feature (see figure 5.7). You can also add "Collaborators," which would allow for the teacher team to be able to contribute to this board.

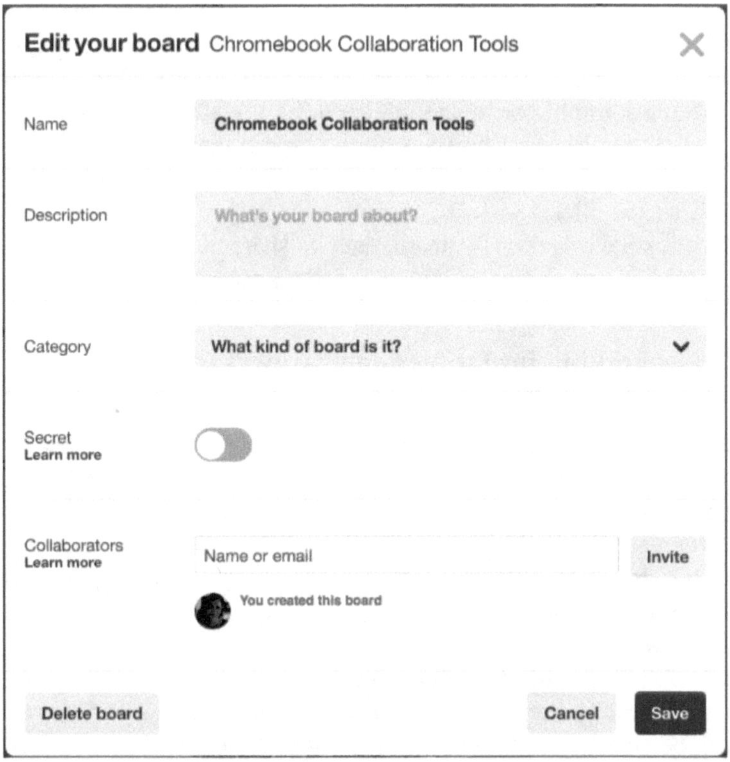

Figure 5.7. Edit Pinterest Board

Now do a Pinterest Search and Save. For Pinterest searches, you want to use shorter terms as keywords such as "chromebooks collaboration," "K12 collaboration," "collaboration tools," "Google collaboration tools," "chromebooks," and "collaboration." Note that at the top of the Pinterest search results, you have options to filter your results: All Pins, Your Pins, Buyable Pins, People, and Boards. Over time, explore all of these filters (see figure 5.8).

Figure 5.8. Pinterest Search and Filters

Click a resource you want to review and vet and if you find something you want to save, click "Save" in the upper left. You will be asked to "Choose board," so select the board you want to add your resource to and select "Save."

Next do a Google Search with Save to Pinterest. Open a new tab in your browser and do a Google Search on your topic. Remember that Pinterest browser button you added when you set up Pinterest? See point 3 in the section above, "Get Started with Pinterest." When you find a resource you like, you can now add it to Pinterest *if* the page has a graphic or image. Pinterest is a graphic and image-centric tool and calls these images "Pins." If the page does not have a graphic or image, it cannot be saved to Pinterest.

Next, click the Pinterest browser button, and if there are relevant graphics or images (Pins), choose your favorite image/Pin from the ones that Pinterest identifies and click "Save." Choose the board you created, hover over the title, and click Save again. If you are ready to share the board with your teachers, select the Board and copy the URL for sharing, or use the Share feature.

Skill 3: Networking for Professional Growth

Along with being a resourceful instructional leader, George Couros (2012) said that building relationships is the most important thing he does as a division principal. A school leader must both personally build relationships and also support others in the learning community to build relationships. One way this can be done is by focusing on networking for professional growth. Networking for professional growth has been gaining traction with the concept of developing personal learning environments (PLEs) and personal learning networks (PLNs).

Your PLE consists of your tools and your knowledge of how to use them. Google searches, Twitter, Facebook, and Pinterest are now part of your PLE. PLEs can be customized to meet your needs and are powerful for learning on your own. Combine your PLE with people, collaborations, and relationships, and voila! Welcome to your PLN! Think about the Twitter users, Facebook friends, and Pinterest pinners you have been encountering. Your PLN allows you to network and exchange ideas with others to further your learning and professional growth.

PLNs have always existed. At a basic level, a PLN includes the resources and the people that help inform one's interests and profession. Most people have always had favorite places to go to and favorite people to call on to find information they need. Consider libraries and librarians, bookstores, specialty stores, museums, and colleagues. One superintendent noted of a trusted colleague, "I called him because it was cheaper than using an attorney. . . . I wasn't afraid to pick the phone up, and I still call him at times" (McClellan, Ivory, & Domínguez, 2008, p. 351).

The modern web has multiplied the possibilities for networking and accessing resources to solve the problems that exist right now. With access to the Internet—with a world of information and a global community at our fingertips—"we can start to create a personal learning network—a set of connections to people and resources both online and offline who enrich our learning—at a moment's notice" (Richardson & Mancabelli, 2011, p. 2).

Warlick (2009) illustrates such a "moment's notice" scenario and explains how he tapped into his online connections as he was writing an article about PLNs:

> As I wrote this article in a local coffee shop, I posted the following message on Twitter: "Writing article about PLN. What's your favorite PLN tool—besides Twitter?" Over the next two hours, 33 Twitter-using educators from across the United States suggested such tools as Skype, Google Reader, Second Life, Mailing Lists, Diigo, Ning, Delicious, Google Talk, wikis, and blogs.

Warlick's (2009) scenario includes another overwhelming list of tools. To narrow this list down, two tools from your toolkit—Twitter and Facebook—will be discussed further in this section and used later in your next administrative scenario. Though Facebook is not on Warlick's list, it is useful. Twitter and Facebook are excellent starting tools for you because (a) the education community is highly active in these tools, and (b) they represent the best of both PLEs and PLNs, as you can learn on your own or you can network and exchange ideas with others.

Tools like Twitter and Facebook are increasingly being used for supplementing and even replacing traditional professional development. Garland (2012) writes,

> Twitter and Facebook might soon replace traditional professional development for teachers. Instead of enduring hours-long workshops a few times a year, teachers could reach out to peers on the Internet in real time for advice on things

like planning a lesson (or salvaging a lesson that's going wrong), overcoming classroom management problems, or helping students with disabilities. (para. 1)

Twitter has its supporters and critics, but, overall, more and more educators are turning to Twitter for its ease of use and as a quick way to network with other like-minded educators from around the world. Boss (2008) describes one teacher's professional development experience with Twitter:

> He's found it especially useful for learning how to integrate podcasting, blogs, wikis, and other tools in his classroom. And if he runs into a challenge, he knows right where to turn for help. "I can watch and learn from people who jump out and try things early," he says. "Once I gather information from observing, then I'm ready to apply it myself in my situation. Watch, observe, apply. It's been great." (para. 16)

This quotation illustrates both the type of learning experience that a school leader needs to understand for personal use and the perspective of an instructional leader who is modeling the experience for teachers.

Building on this perspective, Jane Hart has written an excellent web post titled, "The Web Is 25 Years Old Today—So How Has It Changed the Way We Learn?" She notes,

> I talk a lot about the importance of professional social networking and usually mention how I couldn't do my own work nowadays without Twitter, but there is usually someone who points out that you can't learn to become a doctor using Twitter. And of course this is true—but it's actually missing the point. It's not about using Twitter to learn how to become a doctor, but about using Twitter to become a better doctor—or certainly a better-informed doctor, and keep up to date with what's new in the medical profession. (Hart, 2014b, para. 6)

Hart calls this "learning the new" and further describes the phenomenon as follows:

> Learning the new is, however, a very different learning experience from learning in a traditional training (or e-learning) event—where the content has been organised, structured, and "packaged" up for delivery in a very prescribed way. Learning the new involves being in the flow of new ideas and "joining the dots" between unstructured pieces of knowledge that are encountered. So for those who have been using the Web—and particularly the Social Web for many years—learning will never be the same again. (2014b, para. 7)

In a graduate learning design and technology classes, students develop their PLNs and use discussion forums to engage in reflection about the process. The following is from a student who gave permission to share her reflection on how she focused on Twitter as she built her PLN.

> Connecting with others of similar interests around the world is simple, if one is willing to put in the work. The most common way to connect is through websites like Twitter, which is the "backbone" for the majority of PLNs (Whitby, 2013). By using hashtags, teachers can find common subject teachers. . . . Personally, I am going to use twitter hashtags to start following people as well as look for blogs.
> I am only in my fifth year of teaching, and I know that I can learn vastly from my colleagues. Building a PLN will help me grow as a teacher, reflect as an educator, and influence others. In this connected, networked world, it is crucial that we are always committed to improve[ing] our craft, never becoming complacent with our profession. . . .
> Twitter offers valuable methods for educators to connect through Tweets, hashtags, and lists. When searching for people . . . to follow, I searched hashtags to find teachers with similar interests. Twitter allows participants to have "instant, anytime access to their PLN" and have meaningful conversations with passionate educators (Lalonde, 2012).
> Twitter can be used to share ideas, pose questions, and to give insight on content knowledge, educational technology, and classroom management. Twitter chats are a great way to learn about trends in education and find resources to bring back to the classroom. I am most looking forward to obtaining more lab ideas, as one can never have enough, and I like changing my activities each year. (Personal communication, January 30, 2015)

Facebook combines both personal and professional networking and if used strategically, it is a powerful tool for your PLN. Another student developed his PLN in one of the previously noted graduate learning design and technology classes and was excited to share his PLN story, specifically his use of Facebook, and gave permission to share it with you. His career goal was to be a zookeeper—and the good news is, as this article was being written, he noted that he was a zookeeper in a major city zoo. He said,

> In the zoo community, everyone has the same basic qualifications. Everyone has a four-year degree and limited experience. Facebook has been a great addition to my PLN. There is a group on Facebook called Zookeepers that is only for people in the zoo community (i.e. zookeepers, volunteers, people who are studying to be zookeepers, etc.) and when I joined in Summer 2013 there were about 1100 people in it. There are now over 7000 members from all over the world. I can contact zookeepers in the UK, Europe, Australia, Canada, and America. The expanse of their knowledge is endless.
> I am a fairly new zookeeper who still has a lot to learn, so when I come across something I don't know the answer to, I can post it in the group and get an answer almost immediately. For example, just recently we had a parrot that

was in poor health. I had never worked with an exotic bird like this, so I posted my questions and concerns in the group. By the end of the day, I had over 75 responses from 50 different people. It was a tremendous help.

Another example—I recently went on a trip to Kansas, and went to the Topeka Zoo. I posted in the Zookeepers group asking if there were any keepers from the Topeka Zoo and I was able to contact the elephant manager who then gave me a private tour, answered a ton of questions about the care and training of their animals, allowed me to feed a hippopotamus and a giraffe, and get within 3 feet of a sloth! Now, we are friends on Facebook, and she is going to contact me when they are in a nearby city to pick up one of their elephants so that I can come up and help them with the transport.

This is an incredible opportunity for me that I wouldn't have had without developing and maintaining my PLN! Online networking is just as important as any other way of networking. And it can expand your PLN more than you know. (Personal communication, January 30, 2015)

This is an excellent story to share with anyone who wonders about Facebook as a place for professional networking and growth. Further, the author shares her experiences with Facebook, as it is a source for trending topics and breaking news, both personally and professionally. In addition, she can share, interact, and network with favorite people. Here is how it works:

- Choose to be "Friends" with knowledgeable professional colleagues who share current and vetted resources, including personal experiences and opinions about these resources;
- "Like" the pages of the people, top organizations, and groups in relevant fields, and all of the top research and breaking news is pulled directly into one's feed;
- "Share" experiences and opinions about favorite current and vetted resources;
- Use the Comment, Posting, and Messaging features to further interact and network as needed; and
- Create pages and groups as needed. The author has a private and public page, has created a Facebook page for the family store, created groups for select classes, and a group for a recent grant-funded project with administrators and group leaders.

Administrative Scenario: Networking for Professional Growth

And now, for the last time, you return back to the scenario. In one week, you are scheduled to join your team of teachers participating in an upcoming pilot to deploy one-to-one Chromebook use in their classrooms during fall semester. Remember that they are engaging in professional development about using collaborative tools and increasing collaborative teamwork in their classrooms with the Chromebooks. You are still developing your skills with new tools, along with searching and curating skills.

This week, you are headed to a conference where you will attend workshops and network with other administrators and educators who are also implementing one-to-one Chromebook programs. With your new toolkit and skills, you realize that you have an opportunity to build your personal learning network in a meaningful way, extending and fully taking advantage of the relationships and real-life scenarios of those doing the same things you are doing. The first thing you want to do is identify and participate in the preconference activities:

1. Based on your current skill set, identify and do a Twitter search on the related conference hashtag and follow the conference Twitter account. Join or like the related Facebook page.
2. It is possible to "virtually meet" people in Twitter and Facebook and add new Twitter and Facebook contacts to your PLN. You will see that there are people who are posting with the related hashtag/s or posting on the Facebook page. Click on those people. If they are contributing in ways that appeal to you, follow them, reply to them, like their posts, and so on.
3. It is also possible to make plans before you even leave for the conference. If you use Twitter to set up meetings, they are called "tweetups."
4. Create or find an existing list for this group of Twitter users. Remember: to do this, you click on your own name to go to your Home page, select Lists, and select Create a list.

During the conference, continue to use the conference hashtag to "virtually meet" people and then try to meet them IRL (in real life) and vice versa. When you meet people IRL, find out the best way to stay connected. By following the conference hashtag, you can learn a lot of behind-the-scenes information, sometimes referred to as a "backchannel." Further interact by creating your own Facebook posts and tweets to help you reflect and share. Reply, Retweet, and Like your favorite tweets from others. Like, Comment, and Save Facebook posts. After the conference, interact with and maintain your new connections.

And finally, when you attend your meeting with your teachers, you will be able to talk the talk! You will have the vocabulary, tools, skills, and resources to fulfill your role as instructional leader.

CONCLUSION

After three weeks, if you stick with it for just 15 to 30 minutes a day, you will soon begin to feel comfortable with powerful online tools—Google Search,

Twitter, Facebook, and Pinterest—along with the key skills of searching, curating, and networking. You will find yourself showing and sharing with others how they too, can Google, tweet, post on Facebook, and Pin it! If you need help, you can find the author and her PLN at http://juliaparra.com.

REFERENCES

Bhaskar K, S. (2013). Improve your PLN—Must-know Twitter hashtags for administrators. *EdTechReview*. Retrieved from http://edtechreview.in/e-learning/711-improve-your-pln-must-know-twitter-hashtags-for-administrators

Boss, S. (2008, August 13). Twittering, not frittering: Professional development in 140 characters. *Edutopia*. George Lucas Educational Foundation. Retrieved from http://www.edutopia.org/twitter-professional-development-technology-microblogging

Couros, G. (2012). 21st-Century PLNs for school leaders. *Edutopia*. George Lucas Educational Foundation. Retrieved from http://www.edutopia.org/blog/21st-century-PLNs-school-leaders-george-couros

Davis, V. (2015). 20 top Pinterest tips. *Edutopia*. George Lucas Educational Foundation. Retrieved from http://www.edutopia.org/blog/20-top-pinterest-tips-vicki-davis

EDUCAUSE. (2012). Seven things you should know about social content and curation. *EDUCAUSE Learning Initiative (ELI)*. Retrieved from http://www.educause.edu/library/resources/7-things-you-should-know-about-social-content-curation

Garland, S. (2012, August 1). Can Twitter replace traditional professional development? The HechingerEd blog. *Teachers College at Columbia University*. Retrieved from http://hechingered.org/content/can-twitter-replace-traditional-professional-development_5315/

Hart, J. (2014a). 2014 Top 100 Tools for Learning. *Centre for Learning and Performance Technologies*. Retrieved from http://c4lpt.co.uk/top100tools/

Hart, J. (2014b). The Web is 24 years old today—so how has it changed the way we learn? Retrieved from http://www.c4lpt.co.uk/blog/2014/03/12/the-web-is-25-years-old-today/

Heick, T. (2013). The 4 principle of digital literacy. Retrieved from http://www.teachthought.com/technology/4-principals-of-digital-literacy/

Lalonde, C. (2012, September). How important is Twitter in your personal learning network? *eLearn Magazine: Education and Technology in Perspective*. Retrieved from http://elearnmag.acm.org/archive.cfm?aid=2379624

McClellan, R., Ivory, G., & Domínguez, R. (2008). Distribution of influence, communication, and relational mentoring in the U.S. superintendency. *Mentoring & Tutoring: Partnership in Learning, 16*(3), 346–358.

National Policy Board for Educational Administration (2015). *Professional Standards for Educational Leaders 2015*. Retrieved from http://www.wallacefoundation.org/knowledge-center/Documents/Professional-Standards-for-Educational-Leaders-2015.pdf

Patterson, J. L. (1993). *Leadership for tomorrow's schools.* Alexandria, VA: Association for Supervision and Curriculum Development.

Richardson, W., & Mancabelli, R. (2011). *Personal learning networks: Using the power of connections to transform education.* Bloomington, IN: Solution Tree Press.

Warlick, D. (2009). Grow your personal learning network: New technologies can keep you connected and help you manage information overload. *Learning & Leading with Technology, 36*(6), 12–16.

Whitaker, B. (1997). Instructional leadership and principal visibility. *The Clearing House: A Journal of Educational Strategies, Issues and Ideas, 70*(3), 155–156.

Whitby, T. (2013, November 8). How do I get a PLN? Retrieved from http://www.edutopia.org/blog/how-do-i-get-a-pln-tom-whitby?utm_source=facebook&utm_medium=post&utm_campaign=blog-whitby-pln-shared-image-ocean-quote-venspired

Willison, R. (2008). What makes an instructional leader. *Scholastic Administrator.* Retrieved from http://www.scholastic.com/browse/article.jsp?id=3748622

Chapter Six

Legal Issues for Educators in Using Technology and Social Media

Robert F. Hachiya

KEY POINTS IN THIS CHAPTER

- This chapter is intended as informational on the topic of legal issues and technology for principals and is not legal advice. If you are seeking legal advice, you should consult a licensed attorney in your state.
- Social media can empower school employees, but employees can also use them to communicate a message that results in endangering their careers.
- Courts weigh citizens' rights to free speech against employer rights to maintain a workforce that is acceptable to the profession and the community.
- Social media posts from even the distant past can have negative effects on an employee's relationship with the employee's district.
- Following the advice at the end of this chapter will help you avoid career problems because of your social media use.

Although "technology" and "social media" have separate meanings, the terms are often used interchangeably. Frequently when teachers refer to using "technology" in their classroom, they are referring to the nearly limitless possibilities of educational apps and programs that they can use with students. Such use is part of the transformative and positive results of increased advancements and technological change. Social media is also used in the classroom but is more likely to be used on a personal, non-school-related basis by both teachers and students.

Principals must be concerned not only with policy surrounding district-owned devices but also with policy regarding personally owned devices brought to campus. Rapid advancements in technology arrive at a pace seemingly faster than school policy can be formulated in response to them.

Of perhaps the greatest concern for educators is personal behavior on social media that is deemed inappropriate by employers. Adults working in schools face the very real issue of blurred lines among (a) protected speech while speaking as a private citizen, (b) nonprotected speech while serving in the capacity of a school employee, and (c) behavior conducted by someone who must adhere to community standards.

Social media makes varieties of speech extremely common and in many cases potentially hazardous to the career of an educator. Misuse of social media by teachers is often well publicized, given teachers are often held to higher moral standards than the general population (Fulmer, 2010). This potential problem is further complicated by the fact that it is commonplace for employees to have private social media contact with fellow employees as well as with their supervisors (O'Connor & Schmidt, 2015).

SOCIAL MEDIA AND THE SPEECH RIGHTS OF EDUCATORS

Because public school teachers and principals are school employees, there are important considerations that relate to the regulation of speech, whether or not technology is involved. However, the use of social media creates a potential danger zone for school employees. Educators must be aware that there are limitations to what they should post on social media related to their job, their employer, school district policies, and even current world events.

POLITICAL OR POLICY COMMENTARY ON SOCIAL MEDIA

Similar to students, school employees, including principals and teachers, do not lose their constitutional rights at the schoolhouse gate. The authority to regulate teacher and principal expression combined with the extensive public nature of social media and other online activity creates tension between the speech rights of educators and those who wish to regulate that speech. Although educators and other public sector employees have more protections than most private sector employees, most states provide little protection to workers punished for their online postings (Stoss, 2007).

The worldwide spread of the digital public square creates challenges for both employers and employees. Private sector employees have almost no First Amendment protection, since in general such employees are hired and fired at will. Private employers have the right to determine if social media conduct is harassing or discriminatory, or whether the online activity affects the employment relationship or company values.

However, because First Amendment protections relate to government regulation of speech, public school employers and employees are considered government actors who have speech rights with limitations. The U.S. Supreme Court affirmed the First Amendment speech rights of all public employees, including teachers, in a case that centered on a teacher who publicly criticized his school district in a letter to the editor of his local newspaper (*Pickering v. Board of Education*, 1968).

The Supreme Court later recognized, in 1977, that there could be other reasons to discipline teachers who were exercising their constitutional rights (*Mt. Healthy City Bd. of Ed. v. Doyle*, 1977). Furthermore, the First Amendment does not protect a public employee airing personal grievances, which might well include those aired on social media (*Connick v. Myers*, 1983).

In the *Pickering* case, a balancing test was created to affirm that teachers preserved the right to speak on issues of public importance without risk of losing their job. The court noted the need to "arrive at a balance between the interests of the teacher, as a citizen, in commenting upon matters of public concern, and the interest of the State, as an employer, in promoting the efficiency of the public services it performs through its employees" (*Pickering v. Board of Education*, 1968, p. 568).

This test was modified in 2006 when the U. S. Supreme Court stated, "When public employees make statements pursuant to their official duties, the employees are not speaking as citizens for First Amendment purposes, and the Constitution does not insulate their communications from employer discipline" (*Garcetti v. Ceballos*, 2006, p. 421). While *Garcetti* expressly refused to apply the doctrine to educational settings and academic freedom, the extent of the ruling on schools is substantial (Bathon & Brady, 2010).

When teachers and principals speak in their capacity and function as employees, even through social media, they are subject to increased regulation. When they speak and conduct activities as private citizens away from the boundaries of the school, they are subject to less regulation. However, the lines can become very blurred because of the public nature of social media.

There is no clear, bright line between when a principal or teacher is speaking solely as a private citizen and when that principal or teacher is not speaking as a private citizen. Therefore, educators who use social media to comment on political matters, school policy, or other social commentary must be diligent in protecting themselves from negative employment consequences.

Educators posting on social media sites, even from personally owned devices, writing off-campus and off-duty, could still be subject to disciplinary actions by employers. School boards have the authority to uphold what they believe are higher moral standards and appropriate community standards, and educators have lost their jobs for "conduct unbecoming a teacher" or "unfitness" as defined in some state statutes (Imber, Van Geel, Blokhuis, & Feldman, 2014).

Typically, there should be no expectation of privacy using district-supplied technology. Commonly, the act of logging on a device or network requires your acknowledgment that you agree to usage parameters and a diminished expectation of privacy. Email and texts on public-school-supplied devices are covered by state public-records laws, and while some are exempt from disclosure, there are limited exceptions.

It is also important to recognize that what everyone has posted is likely "out there" forever, regardless of whether you have deleted it. Email can also mistakenly be sent to unintended recipients or can be forwarded by anyone after it is sent, a practice the original sender has no control over.

With the use of social media, a moment of indiscretion can potentially ruin a career. Examples are common including the firing of a teacher for sending racially charged tweets (Gallman, 2015); a personal blog calling students "dunderhead" and "whiny, simpering grade-grubber" (Walsh, 2015); or a headline-making case like the firing of a teacher who posted on Facebook that one of her activities was "teaching chitlins in the ghetto of Charlotte" and that she taught "in the most ghetto school in Charlotte" (Helms, 2008).

While a strong case can be made for discipline against teachers and principals who post racist or demeaning messages, there are other examples where the line is not so clear-cut. Here are two examples: The first involves a 24-year-old teacher who was pressured to resign after parents complained about pictures she had posted on Facebook of her European vacation. The pictures showed her holding alcoholic beverages and included a statement that she was headed to "Crazy Bitch Bingo" (AJC, 2010). The second is a student-teacher dismissed from her student teaching position after it was discovered her MySpace profile included a picture of her wearing a pirate cap and drinking from a plastic cup that was captioned "Drunken Pirate" (*Snyder v. Millersville University*, 2008).

Although there can be a healthy debate surrounding the ethics involved with monitoring teacher social media, there is no question that teachers expose themselves to potential risk when they have a social media presence. The NEA in *Tomorrow's Teachers* cites examples of aspiring teachers not getting jobs due to Facebook postings that referenced their drinking, sexual activities, and derogatory comments about their students (Simpson, 2015). A growing number of school districts monitor social media with the specific intent to find inappropriate online postings and other content by teachers (Bathon & Brady, 2010).

SUGGESTED POLICY AND PRACTICE RELATED TO EDUCATORS AND SOCIAL MEDIA

In matters related to technology policies, it is imperative to follow all laws and local school board policy. Some districts, for example, may have far more stringent rules governing staff use of social media than others do. Some districts may encourage the use of social media while others prohibit it. The bottom line is to know your own local policies and regulations.

Common sense dictates that there is no expectation of privacy when posting on any form of social media, regardless of the privacy settings the platform may have. Everything that is posted is searchable by anyone, including school board members, coworkers, parents, students, the media, and the general public.

ADVICE REGARDING PROFESSIONAL AND PERSONAL SOCIAL MEDIA

- If you choose to use social media, have a minimum of two social media profiles (accounts), a professional profile and personal one. Never conduct social media activity that blends the two together.
- Understand the social media that you use. Not understanding how the platform or application works can lead to irreversible mistakes. Nearly every social media platform provides extensive tutorials regarding its functions, as well as guidelines for appropriate activity.
- Review and, if necessary, cleanse your personal social media presence if you have not done so. Do this especially when job searching, since some employers examine social media during the hiring process.
- Do not identify your school or school district on your personal profile.
- Never use devices owned or provided by a school district for any personal social media activity.
- Always remember that comments and postings both online and offline made in the capacity of a teacher or principal are not protected speech.
- While educators should not feel compelled to suppress their speech, they ought to use discretion and common sense. Understand the general differences between speaking as a citizen and speaking as an employee.
- Even if you are clearly acting as a private citizen, your social media postings could still place you in jeopardy if such postings are deemed inappropriate or place your employer in a negative light.
- Do not post anything on social media that you would not share with your human resources department, your boss, your coworkers, your family, or the public.

- Do not post anything that could demean or degrade the profession or any individual.
- A social media presence that includes personal photographs depicting anything remotely controversial could place you at risk. Such controversies are not limited to just politics and religion but essentially any topic on which there may be differing viewpoints.
- Teachers and principals should keep their personal social media profiles private. Exercise extreme caution when considering "friending" parents on your personal social media.
- Local policy or even state law could prohibit social media communication with students, but even if such communication is allowed, exercise discretion. Never engage with students on personal social media.
- If social media is used for educational purposes, keep communications with students public, using a specific school-related platform.
- Take every measure to comply with student-privacy laws when using all social media but especially when using school social media accounts.

Even though new technology can create changes faster than educators sometimes think they can keep pace with, the truth is that when you exercise good judgment, common sense, and discretion, there shouldn't be many problems that outweigh the benefits that advanced technology can bring to students, staff, and schools.

CONCLUSION

While the advancement of technology has positives for students and teachers alike, new technology is almost always accompanied by new ways to misuse or abuse it. Educators using technology and social media, whether for professional or personal use, must be mindful of their responsibilities and obligations related to that use. Educators also have significant responsibilities related to the student use of technology and social media, and they must ensure that they protect their own welfare and that of their students.

REFERENCES

AJC. (2010). Barrow teacher fired over Facebook still not back in classroom. Retrieved from http://www.ajc.com/news/news/local/barrow-teacher-fired-over-facebook-still-not-back-/nQmpS/#__federated=1

Bathon, J. M., & Brady, K. P. (2010). Teacher free speech and expression in a digital age: A legal analysis. *NASSP Bulletin*, *94*(3), 213–226. Retrieved from ProQuest Research Library.

Connick v. Myers, 461 U.S. 138 (1983).

Fulmer, E. H. (2010). Privacy expectations and protections for teachers in the Internet age. *Duke Law and Technology Review*, *9*, 1–31.

Gallman, S. (2015). Texas teacher fired after Ferguson tweets. Retrieved from CNN website: http://www.cnn.com/2014/11/14/us/texas-teacher-fired-ferguson-tweet/index.html?hpt=hp_t2

Garcetti v. Ceballos, 547 U.S. 410, 126 S. Ct. 1951, 164 L. Ed. 2d 689 (2006).

Helms, A. (2008). Charlotte teachers face actions because of Facebook postings. *The Charlotte Observer*. Retrieved from http://www.heraldonline.com/news/local/article12241319.html

Imber, M., Van Geel, T., Blokhuis, J. C., & Feldman, J. (2014). *Education law*. 5th ed. New York: Routledge.

Mt. Healthy City Bd. of Ed. v. Doyle, 429 U.S. 274, 97 S. Ct. 568, 50 L. Ed. 2d 471 (1977).

O'Connor, K., & Schmidt, G. (2015). "Facebook fired": Legal standards for social media–based terminations of K-12 public school teachers. *Sage Open*, *5*(1). Retrieved from http://dx.doi.org/10.1177/2158244015575636

Pickering v. Board of Ed. of Township High School Dist. 205, Will Cty., 391 U.S. 563, 88 S. Ct. 1731, 20 L. Ed. 2d 811 (1968).

Simpson, M. (2015). *Social networking nightmares*. Retrieved from http://www.nea.org/home/38324.htm

Snyder v. Millersville University, Civil Action. No. 07-1660 (E.D. Pa. Dec. 3, 2008).

Stoss, R. (2007, December 30). How to lose your job on your own time. *The New York Times*. Retrieved from http://www.nytimes.com/2007/12/30/business/30digi.html

Walsh, M. (2015). Teacher's blog posts slamming students not protected, judge rules. *Education Week—The School Law Blog*. Retrieved from http://blogs.edweek.org/edweek/school_law/2014/07/teachers_blog_posts_slamming_s.html?utm_source=feedblitz&utm_medium=FeedBlitzRss&utm_campaign=theschoollawblog

Glossary

Browser: A computer program that "talks" to a server to find web pages on the Internet or to access sites and information on a network (Orgera, 2016).

BYOD (Bring Your Own Device): A system where digital devices would not only be purchased by the school district but students would also have the option to use their own smartphones and tablet computers to complete classwork or access learning resources while at school (Room 241 Team, 2012).

Curation: A field of endeavor involved with assembling, managing, and presenting some type of collection (Rouse, 2017a).

Digital literacy: Reading and writing skills using technology (Heitin, 2016). There are five kinds:

1. Photovisual literacy is the ability to read and deduce information from visuals.
2. Reproduction literacy is the ability to use digital technology to create a new piece of work or combine existing pieces of work together to make it your own.
3. Branching literacy is the ability to successfully navigate in the nonlinear medium of digital space.
4. Information literacy is the ability to search, locate, assess, and critically evaluate information found on the web and on-shelf in libraries.
5. Socioemotional literacy refers to the social and emotional aspects of being present online, whether it may be through socializing and collaborating, or simply consuming content (Aviram & Eshet-Alkalai, 2006).

Google Chrome Browser: One tool you use to access the Internet. Other tools will most likely be Internet Explorer, Mozilla Firefox, or Apple Safari (Internet Browsers, n.d.).

Google Docs: A free, web-based application in which documents can be created, edited, and stored online. Files can be accessed from any computer with an Internet connection and a full-featured web browser. Google Docs is a part of a comprehensive package of online applications offered by and associated with Google (Rouse, 2017b).

Google Drive: A beefed-up version of Google Docs that allows users to share documents, spreadsheets, and slideshows with submission ability, collaboration, and feedback. You can store your documents, photos, music, videos, and other media all in one place. It syncs with your mobile devices and your computer, so if you make a change from one gadget, the change will automatically show up if you access it elsewhere (Horn, 2012).

Google Forms: An application that provides a fast way to create online surveys, with responses collected in an online spreadsheet. Survey questions can be answered from almost any web browser, including mobile smartphone and tablet browsers (Wolber, 2012).

Google Search: A tool that allows the user to find the answer to a question. Google Search checks billions of web pages, and Google's ranking systems sort through those web pages to give the user a useful and relevant list of results in a fraction of a second ("How Search Algorithms Work," n.d.).

Integrated technology: The integration into normal day-to-day operations of technology relevant to meeting the needs of the organization. Such integration has the potential to improve efficiency and effectiveness.

Phablet: A smartphone that is very large and verges on tablet size such as iPhone 6+ or Samsung Galaxy S®5 ("Phablet: Phone Tablet Hybrid," n.d.).

Pinterest: A visual bookmarking tool that allows users to explore and save (i.e., "pin") creative ideas for later reference (Pinterest, 2017).

QR (Quick Response) code: A two-dimensional square barcode with embedded links to information such as texts, emails, websites, and phone numbers, that can be read using smartphones or other devices that are compatible with QR reading ("What Is a QR Code?" n.d.).

Skype: A software that allows people to communicate via text, voice, and/or video over the Internet (Skype, 2017).

Social media: "The collective of online communications channels dedicated to community-based input, interaction, content-sharing and collaboration. Websites and applications dedicated to forums, microblogging, social networking, social bookmarking, social curation, and wikis are among the different types of social media" (Rouse, 2016a).

Tablet: A wireless, portable personal computer with a touchscreen interface. The tablet is typically smaller than a notebook computer, but larger than a smartphone (Rouse, 2016b).

Website: A connected group of pages on the World Wide Web regarded as a single entity, usually maintained by one person or organization and devoted to a single topic or several closely related topics ("Website," n.d.).

YouTube: A free video-sharing website that makes it easy to watch online videos. You can even create and upload your own videos to share with others. Originally created in 2005, YouTube is now one of the most popular sites on the web, with visitors watching around six billion hours of video every month (GCF Global, 2017).

REFERENCES

Aviram, A., & Eshet-Alkalai, Y. (2006). Towards a theory of digital literacy: Three scenarios for the next steps. *European Journal of Open, Distance and E-Learning*. Retrieved from http://www.eurodl.org/index.php?p=archives&year=2006&halfyear=1&abstract=223

GCF Global. (2017). YouTube: What is YouTube? Retrieved from https://www.gcflearnfree.org/youtube/what-is-youtube/1/

Heitin, L. (2016). What is digital literacy? Retrieved from *Education Week*: http://www.edweek.org/ew/articles/2016/11/09/what-is-digital-literacy.html

Horn, L. (2012). What is Google Drive? Retrieved from Gizmodo: http://gizmodo.com/5904653/what-is-google-drive

How search algorithms work. (n.d.). Retrieved from https://www.google.com/search/howsearchworks/algorithms/

Internet browsers. (n.d.). Retrieved from https://www.taskstream.com/Main/Help2/LAT/coordinator_web/Content/FAQs/SystemRequFAQs/Whatbrowser.htm

Orgera, S. (2016). What is a web browser? Web browsers and how they work. Retrieved from Lifewire: https://www.lifewire.com/what-is-a-browser-446234

Phablet: Phone tablet hybrid. (n.d.). In *Webopedia*. Retrieved from https://www.webopedia.com/TERM/P/phablet.html

Pinterest. (2017). Retrieved from https://www.pinterest.com/

Room 241 Team. (2012). What is BYOD (Bring Your Own Device) and why should teachers care? Retrieved from Room 241: http://education.cu-portland.edu/blog/tech-ed/what-is-byod-bring-your-own-device-and-why-should-teachers-care/

Rouse, M. (2016a). Social media. Retrieved from TechTarget: http://whatis.techtarget.com/definition/social-media

Rouse, M. (2016b). Tablet. In *SearchMobileComputing*. Retrieved from http://searchmobilecomputing.techtarget.com/definition/tablet-PC

Rouse, M. (2017a). Curation. Retrieved from TechTarget: https://whatis.techtarget.com/definition/curation

Rouse, M. (2017b). Google Docs. Retrieved from http://whatis.techtarget.com/definition/Google-Docs
Skype. (2017). Retrieved from https://www.skype.com/en/
Website. (n.d.). In Dictionary.com.
What is a QR code? (n.d.) Retrieved from http://www.whatisaqrcode.co.uk/
Wolber, A. (2012). Use Google Forms to create a survey. Retrieved from TechRepublic: http://www.techrepublic.com/blog/google-in-the-enterprise/use-google-forms-to-create-a-survey/

Index

accountability: leadership and, xv, xviii; public demand for, 39; student assessment, 11–12.
Alsbury, Thomas, xix, 39–53
Anderson, S., xv, 11
anxiety, teachers and, 1–2, 7
Apple, x, 10, 12, 14. *See also* iPad
assessments: administrative, 18, 22, 85; learning assessments, 9–12, 18, 22; student assessments, 10–12, 18.
Atkinson, Linda, xix, 25–37
ATLAS.ti software, 9–10, 13–23; for the iPad, 14–16; primary document screen, 15. *See also* CAQDAS
Aviram, A., 85

Badgett, Kevin, xviii, 1–7, 62
Ballenger, Julia W., 93
Barney, H., 11
Bathon, J. M., 79, 80
Bauer, S. C., 9, 12
Bensley, Roseanne, 93
Bereiter, C., xvi
Berends, M., 9, 11
Bhaskar, K., 59
bicycle technology, ix–xi, 37

blogs, 41, 50–53, 58–59, 69–71, 80, 86
Bolton, R. N., 50
Boriack, A. W., 2
Boss, S., 70
Boudett, K. P., 9
Brady, K. P., 79, 80
branching literacy, 85
Brazer, S. D., 9, 12
browser, 57, 61, 63, 68, 85
bubble students, 36
Building Improvement Team (BIT), 47, 49
Burnham, David, x
BYOD (Bring Your Own Device), 85

Cameron, G., 27
CAQDAS, 10, 13–14, 19, 23. *See also* ATLAS.ti software
Cate, Jean, xix, 25–37
Centre for Learning and Performance Technologies, 58
Cervone, L., 26, 27, 29
Chromebook, 63–66, 68, 72–73
Chrome browser, 57, 63, 86. *See also* Google
City, E. A., 9

Classwalk app: case for walkthroughs, 25–27; creating reports; functions, 27–35; overview, 25, 27; teacher information, 28–29; templates, 29–31; time value, 35–36; using walkthrough data, 35; walkthrough, 32.
cloud-based technology, 14, 39, 46–51, 53. *See also* collaboration
Coburn, C. E., 9
codes, 13–14, 16–17, 19–22
collaboration, 36, 39–42, 46–51, 63–69, 72, 85, 86
communication: case scenario, 50–52; *Classwalk* and, 34–35; iBooks and, 2, 6; importance of, 39–41; school administration and, 41, 52–53; social media and, 57–58, 60, 82, 86.
computer technology, ix–xi, xvii–xviii
Connick v. Myers (1983), 79
Cooper, J., 1
Copland, M. A., 10
Couros, George, 58, 62, 68
curation, 6, 55–56, 66, 85, 86

Darilek, H., 11
data-driven decision-making: ATLAS.ti as support for, 18; overview, 9–10; qualitative side of, 10–11.
David, J., 26
Davis, T., 27
Dean, Sharon, xix, 25–37
decision-making. *See* data-driven decision-making
Dedoose, 10, 13
Dempster, P., 13
Denzin, N. K., 11
determinism, xvii
digital literacy, 85
Dinh, H. T., 48
DuFour, R., 43
dystopianism, xvii

Education Deans for Justice and Equity, xiv

education leadership, xiv–xv
Educlipper, 66
Edutopia, 58, 60, 61
Edwards, C., 27, 29
efficiency, x, xvii, 1–2, 13, 37, 40–43, 46–48, 50–51, 53, 66, 79, 86
Eshet-Alkalai, Y., 85
expertise as a career, defined, xvi

Facebook, 48, 51, 53, 55–56; getting started with, 60–61; networking, 68–69, 71–74; privacy and, 80; searching for information with, 62, 64–65. *See also* social media
Faulds, D. J., 50
First Amendment rights, 78–79
Flanagan, L., 39
Fulmer, E. H., 78

Gallman, S., 80
Garcetti v. Ceballos (2006), 79
Garcia, Krista, 93
Garland, S., 69
Goldring, E., 9, 11
Goodwin, B., 27, 29
Google, 56–59, 61–66, 68–69, 73–74; explanation of tools, 86; Google Forms, 43, 44; Google Scholar, 5; Google Search, 56; Google Street, 45; G Suite, 43, 46, 48.
Greenwood, D., 50
Grissom, J., 26, 35

Hachiya, Robert F., xix, 46, 53, 77–82
Hart, Jane, 70
Heick, T., 66
Heitin, L., 85
Helms, A., 80
Hochhalter, Gina, 93
Horn, L., 86
Hu, W. C., 46
Huberman, A. M., 13

iBooks app: educational value, 2–3; emailing documents from, 5;

PDF documents in, 4–6; saving a document to, 3. *See also* Apple; iPad
Ikemoto, G. S., 11
information literacy, 85
insight, explained, x–xi
integrated technology, 86
International Society for Technology Education (ISTE), 40–41. *See also* technology
interventions, 11, 36
iPad: ATLAS.ti for, 9–10, 12–23; cautions, 6; *Classwalk* app, 25, 27, 34; Internet capabilities, 2–3. *See also* Apple; iBooks

Jacobsen, M., 39
Jensen, E., 36
Jobs, Steve, x

Kachur, D., 27, 29
Kerr, K. A., 11
Khajeh-Hosseni, A., 50
Knapp, M. S., 10
Koppel, Ted, x
Kuo, L. H., 46

Lalonde, C., 71
Language Proficiency Assessment Committee (LPAC), 4
learning assessments, 9–12, 18, 22. *See also* Language Proficiency Assessment Committee
Learnist, 66
Lee, C., 48
Lee, Y. H., 2
legal issues, 77, 79–80
Lehr, M. D., 9
Leithwood, K., xv
Lemke, M., 9
lesson plans, 12, 45
Lester, Jessica N., xviii, 9–23
Lincoln, Y. S., 11
literacy, 26, 28–31, 85
Lloyd, C., 26

Lochmuller, Chad R., xviii, 9–23
Loeb, S., 26, 35
Lovejoy, K., 41
Luo, M., 11

MacNeil, A., 2
Malone, Glenn, 93
Mancabelli, R., 69
Mangold, W. G., 50
Marsh, J. A., 11
Martinez-Miller, P., 26, 27, 29
Marzano, R., 25, 35–36
Master, B., 26, 35
Mattos, M., 43
MAXQDA, 10, 13
McClellan, R., 69
McDonald, Teena, 93
McKenzie, K. B., xiv
McNulty, B., 25, 35
McREL leadership evaluation model, 27, 35–36
memos, 16–17
message boards, 41
Microsoft Office, 14, 16, 23, 43
Miles, M. B., 13
mobile devices, 48, 51, 57, 86
Monpas-Huber, J., 10
Mt. Healthy City Bd. of Ed. v. Doyle (1977), 79
Murname, R. J., 9

Nash, John, ix–xi, 37
National Education Policy Center, xiii
NEA (National Education Association), 80
networking, 55–56, 58–60; professional growth, 68–74, 80. *See also* personal learning networks; social media
Nightline (television program), x
Niyato, D., 48
NVivo, 10, 13

O'Connor, K., 78
online tools, 55
Orgera, S., 85

Pane, J. F., 11
Parra, Julia L., xix, 6, 55–74
Patterson, J. L., 62
Paulus, T., 13
PDF documents, 2, 4, 14, 18, 23, 34
peer-reviewed articles, 1, 5
personal learning environments (PLEs), 55–56, 68–69
personal learning networks (PLNs), 55–56, 69–74
phablets, 57, 63, 86
photovisual literacy, 85
Pickering v. Board of Education (1968), 79
Pinterest, 55–56, 61–62, 66–69, 74, 86
Pitler, H., 27, 29
Polkinghome, D. E., 11, 12
privacy, 59, 72, 78–79, 81–82
private sector employment, 78–79
project files, 14, 16, 19

qualitative data: analyzing, 13; data-driven leadership, 10–11; examples of, 12; overview, 9–10; sources and analysis process, 12–14. *See also* ATLAS.ti; CAQDAS
queries, 13, 16
Quick Response (QR) codes, 44, 46, 86
quotations, 14

racism, 80
reforms, 39
reproduction literacy, 85
Ribeiro, J., 2
Richardson, W., 69
Robinson, V., 26
Roderick, M., 11
Romero, Arsenio, 94
Rouse, M., 85–87
Rowe, K., 26
Ryan, K., 1

Saldaña, J., 13
Sánchez, Steven, 94
Saxton, G. D., 41

Scardamalia, M., xvi
Scheurich, J. J., xiv
Schmidt, G., 78
school board policy, 4, 5, 79, 81
Scoop.it, 66
searching: Google Search, 56–59, 61, 63–64; for information and resources, 62; as key skill, 55, 62, 73–74; for resources for PD meetings, 63; social media, 53, 59, 61, 64–66, 68; using iBooks for, 2, 4.
Seashore Louis, K. S., xv
Simpson, M., 80
Skrla, L., xiv
Skype, 56, 69, 86
Smith, J. W., 50
Snyder v. Millersville University, 80
social determinism, xvii
social media, 41, 46, 48, 50–52, 56; advice regarding, 81–82; defined, 86; political or policy commentary, 78–80; and speech rights of educators, 78; suggested policy and practice, 81. *See also* Facebook; Pinterest; Twitter
social networks. *See* social media
socioemotional literacy, 85
Sommerville, I., 50
Spring, S. D., 9
stakeholders, 10, 23, 39–41, 45–46, 48, 50–52
standardized testing, 9, 11
Storify, 66
Stoss, R., 78
Stout, J., 27, 29
Stringfield, S., 11
SurveyMonkey, 18, 23
Swinnerton, J. A., 10

tablets, 57, 85–87. *See also* iPad; technology
Tarango, Abigail, 94
Tardew, S., 11
Teaching and Learning Department, 22

technology: collaboration and, 46–48; communication and, 39, 53; efficiency tools, 1, 37; limitations of, 6; overcoming resistance to, 1–2; place in education, xvi–xvii; social media and, 77–78, 81–82; technological determinism, xvii–xviii; technological dystopianism, xvii; technological utopianism, xvii; technology leaders, xvii–xviii. *See also* ATLAS.ti; *Classwalk*; cloud technology; iPad; social media

Texas Board of Education, 4
Tienhaara, Jon, xix, 39–53
training, 2, 6–7, 25–26, 36, 39, 46, 70, 72
Tomorrow's Teachers, 80
Tumblr, 51, 66
Turner, E. O., 9
Twitter, 48, 51, 53, 56, 71, 73–74; getting started with, 58–60; as part of administrators' toolkit, 56, 62; professional development and, 69–70; searching, 64–65.

US Department of Education, 58
utopianism, xvii–xviii

Wahlstrom, K. L., xv
walkthroughs, xi, xix, 16, 25, 27, 29, 31; case for, 25–27. *See also Classwalk*

Walsh, M., 80
Wang, P., 48
Warlick, D., 69
Waters, T., 25, 35, 36
Waters, R. D., 41
Waxman, H. C., 2
Wayman, J. C., 9, 11
Web 2.0, 56
web forms, 43–44
websites: defined, 87; sharing/disseminating information via, 36, 51–53.
Webster, M. D., xvii–xviii
Whitaker, B., 62
Whitby, T., 71
Wicks, David, xix, 39–53
Wilbur, Sharon, xix, 25–37
Williams, J., 27
Williams, Leslie, xix, 25–37
Willison, R., 62
Wilson, S. S., ix–x
Wolber, A., 86

Yang, H. H., 46
Yang, H. J., 46
YouTube, 56, 87
Ysseldyke, J., 11
Yu, J. C., 46

Zookeeper Facebook group, 71–72

About the Contributors

Thomas L. Alsbury is professor of Educational Leadership at Seattle Pacific University and president of Balanced Governance Solutions™, a consulting group for improving school governance.

Linda Atkinson, PhD. is the associate director of the University of Oklahoma's K20 Center for Educational and Community Renewal, for K–12 and STEM education partnerships.

Dr. **Kevin Badgett** is associate professor and coordinator for the educational leadership program at the University of Texas of the Permian Basin, in Odessa, Texas.

Dr. **Dana Christman** is associate professor in the Department of Educational Specialties at Austin Peay State University.

Sharon Dean, MS, is currently an associate director for college and career readiness at the University of Oklahoma's K20 Center for Educational and Community Renewal.

Robert F. Hachiya is associate professor in the Educational Leadership Department of the College of Education at Kansas State University.

Gary Ivory is retired from New Mexico State University.

Jessica N. Lester is aassociate professor of inquiry methodology in the School of Education at Indiana University.

Chad R. Lochmiller is associate professor in the Department of Educational Leadership and Policy Studies at Indiana University, Bloomington.

John B. Nash is associate professor and chair of the Department of Educational Leadership Studies at the University of Kentucky.

Dr. **Julia L. Parra** is faculty at New Mexico State University, coordinator for Learning Design & Technology, and director of the Online Teaching & Learning Graduate Certificate Program.

Dr. **Jon Tienhaara** is the superintendent of South Bend School District in South Bend, Washington.

Dr. **David Wicks** is an associate professor and chair of the Digital Education Leadership program in Seattle Pacific University's School of Education.

Dr. **Sharon Wilbur** is the associate director of Leadership Development at the K20 Center for Educational and Community Renewal at the University of Oklahoma.

Leslie Williams, PhD, is the director of the University of Oklahoma's K20 Center for Educational and Community Renewal.

About the Reviewers

Dr. **Julia W. Ballenger** is professor in the Educational Leadership Doctoral Program at Texas A&M University, Commerce. She serves on international, national, and state executive boards.

Roseanne Bensley has more than 35 years in student affairs and career services and in May 2018 completed her PhD in Educational Leadership and Administration from New Mexico State University.

Krista Garcia has been a teacher, academic dean, assistant principal, and principal and is currently the director of Special Education in Northside ISD in San Antonio, Texas.

Gina Hochhalter is an instructor of English at Clovis Community College, Clovis, New Mexico. She holds an EdD in Educational Leadership and Administration from New Mexico State University.

Dr. **Glenn Malone** provides oversight of assessment, accountability, special education, Title I, LAP, and health services in the Puyallup School District, Puyallup, Washington. He has also been an adjunct professor.

Dr. **Teena McDonald** is clinical faculty at Washington State University. She directs the master's programs for educational leadership and is faculty in the state superintendent certification program.

Dr. **Roland Rios** is director of Technology for the Ft. Sam Houston Independent School District in San Antonio, Texas. He has been a math teacher, secondary principal, and assistant principal.

About the Reviewers

Dr. **Arsenio Romero** is superintendent of Deming Public Schools, Deming, New Mexico, and has been an assistant superintendent in curriculum. He holds a doctorate in educational leadership and administration from New Mexico State University.

Dr. **Steven Sánchez** is currently a multiage middle-grades teacher for the Los Lunas Family School, Los Lunas, New Mexico. He has been an interim superintendent, deputy superintendent, and a program director for the National Science Foundation.

Abigail Tarango is director of Special Projects & Strategic Initiatives for the Ysleta Independent School District in El Paso, Texas. She is a doctoral candidate at New Mexico State University.

www.ingramcontent.com/pod-product-compliance
Lightning Source LLC
Chambersburg PA
CBHW030146240426
43672CB00005B/287